RESPONSES TO *A POLITICAL WRITING*

With characteristic flamboyance and slyness and verve, Jeremy Fernando has produced a political theory of Singapore that may properly be called, i.e., that in some sense invents or reinvents, Singaporean Political Theory. A Political Writing is a meditation of and on indirectness from title ("a" political writing — as though this were anything less than an allusively definitive theory of the Singaporean polis!) to concluding poem ("in case" — on the possibility of being, after all and in this city-state of transitions, liminality, uncertainty, infinite fungibility, someone in particular, a certain someone). Though presented as a collection by this exceptionally prolific writer, Fernando's A Political Writing *is, to the contrary and like Singapore itself, an impossible unity, an integral whole of mismatched parts. From Radiohead to curation, the casino that dare not speak its name to Sarah Choo Jing's 'Dancing without Touching', Fernando swirls together an extraordinary mish-mash of near misses that does not try to arrive and yet, like a letter, unfailingly reaches its destination anyhow. "Perhaps though," he writes, "we can only speak as if we can speak of it". It is Singapore itself. This dreamlike text, spinning across worlds, is only "a" political writing in the sense that Singapore — perhaps more than any other polity in modern history — is at once only an "as if" nation-state and the densest imaginable instantiation of the polis form. Not at all without love, Fernando traces this form in the fullness of its unspeakability. How, the book seems to cry, suppose you could know anything at all about the political if you have not first missed understanding Singapore?*

~ Ira Allen, Associate Professor of Rhetoric at Northern Arizona University, author of *Panic Now? Tools for Humanizing*, *The Ethical Fantasy of Rhetorical Theory*, and sundry other works

Jeremy Fernando's political vision is incisive, inventive, and insidious.

~ Neil Murphy, Professor of English & Toh Puan Mahani Idris Daim Chair Professor, Nanyang Technological University; and author of *John Banville*, and *Irish Fiction and Postmodern Doubt*.

COPYRIGHT © Jeremy Fernando 2025

All rights reserved. No part of this publication may be reproduced or utilised in any form or by any means, electronic or mechanical, including photocopying, recording, all by any information storage and retrieval system, without permission in writing from the publishers.

ISBN: 979-8-9913942-7-7

Published by Hidden Hand Press
www.hiddenhandbooks.com

A POLITICAL WRITING

Jeremy Fernando

History is a fairy tale true to its telling.

~ ANDREI CODRESCU

A created thing is never invented and it is never true: it is always and ever itself.

~ FEDERICO FELLINI

It's incredible how easy it is to believe your own stories even when you know how arbitrary they are.

~ SOPHIE CALLE

signs signs signs
2023

VLADIMIR

Writing, like mourning and history, designates the place of an irreplaceable, marks the trace of a disappearance.

~ CHANTAL THOMAS

Weakness is stronger than strength because it leaves room for thought.

~ CATHERINE BREILLAT

I have principles. If you don't like them, I have others.

~ GROUCHO MARX

abandoned to freedom

two systems sounds fine
her handbag tightly clasped said deaf
to you abandoned

to freedom

fifty years divined
yet tremblingly umbrellas disappeared merely three
shy of two score

just so

spectres of one cannot we avert
yet each day wafts freedom unconfined
towards

uncharted skies

still open

on the death penalty —
fragmentary meditations[1]

> *Some lives are grievable, and others are not; the differential allocation of grievability that decides what kind of subject is and must be grieved, and which kind of subject must not, operates to produce and maintain certain exclusionary conceptions of who is normatively human: what counts as a livable life and a grievable death.*
>
> ~ Judith Butler[2]

Perhaps the question is not so much whether or not the death penalty is good. Not so much because it is a moot one — for, most questions of valuation are based on the criteria by which they are measured; thus, have less to do with what is being judged than the one doing the judging — but precisely because *those who are for* and *those who are against* it hinge their argument around the same premise: that *life is sacred*.

Proponents of the death penalty argue that since one has taken a life, one must then pay for it — one must be held accountable, must

---

[1] A version of this work was first published in *Revista Científica de la Facultad de Derecho y Ciencias Sociales y Políticas — Universidad Nacional del Nordeste* (Vol 1, issue 2), 2022.

[2] Judith Butler, *Precarious Life: The Powers of Mourning and Violence*. London: Verso, 2004, xiv.

be made to account for it. And since life is sacred, beyond the realm of the everyday, the quotidian, quite possibly even beyond what can be known — is transcendent, lies in the realm of the metaphysical — there is no other way to balance the books, as it were, than with the life of the one deemed to have first taken life. Where it is two unknowns which cancel each other out — this is also why one can 'pay' for multiple deaths with one's life; not because quantity as such doesn't matter, but that since there is no matter at play, we are no longer in the realm of quantifiability.[3]

---

[3] This could leave us with the — potentially intriguing — question: *what is the weight of a life*? One that cannot be responded to if we treat life as metaphysical; and might result in an even more banal, dehumanising, response if we start to calculate aspects of living, begin to decide, determine even, what *counts* as living and what does not make the grade, if we transform living into nothing more than figures to be entered into the ledger of an accounting spreadsheet.

A third possibility might entail separating *living* from *life*: taking the former as immanent and the latter as transcendent, which would be a step in the direction of many theological positions, particularly those in the Abrahamic vein. Those of a religious bent might argue that this could be the best-approach: to treat what is knowable as knowable, and what is unknowable as a matter of faith. Which would be another way of saying 'count what you can' and 'for what you cannot, take — on trust — that some higher being is keeping score': in other words, « render therefore unto Caesar the things which are Caesar's; and unto God the things that are God's » (*Matthew* 22:22). Others — probably myself included — would say that this might leave us worse-off: for now not only would you have a neo-liberal approach to living, there would always also be a spectre of *life* over-shadowing living, where this unknown lurks in the background, threatening to be an extension-of this accounting-system, often-times spilling over, intruding, into living itself — as exemplified in theocracies, but really even in so-called

Thus, one must die.[4]

Opponents, on the alleged other hand, argue that since life is sacred, one must not take it: and that, as Margaret Atwood elegantly and powerfully argues in *Cat's Eye*, « an eye for an eye only leads to more blindness ».[5] That legally killing someone — momentarily setting aside whether legality makes it legitimate, or whether the act of killing someone continues to reside in some *para*-legal realm (a murder than isn't a murder because it is deemed to not-be so, is not named-as as such, not seen that way in

---

secular states (the fact that it is the sovereign, and only the sovereign, who has the power to *grant clemency* — that is *forgiveness* — in the event of a death sentence marks the disguised presence of the divine at the very heart of the state). Throw in concepts of 'everlasting life' alongside those of 'heaven' and 'hell' and we're basically in a poem by Dante.

[4] Which might well be why many idealist philosophers are such fans of the death penalty: for, they argue that to be a *good citizen* one has to submit oneself to the law all the way to the end: thus, one has to submit one's life itself to the law. And, should one break the law, one should not just resign oneself to the punishment, one should in fact rejoice that one will be punished — for, that would mean that one has finally acknowledged the truth of the law itself.

Oh yes, the state can have its poetic moments too.

For, once again, one has to bear in mind — as Jacques Derrida continues to teach us — just because we've cut-off the heads of kings doesn't mean we've gotten rid of the notion of the *divine origin* of both the state and authority.

[5] Margaret Atwood, *Cat's Eye*. Toronto: McClelland & Stewart, 1989, 427.

the eyes of the law) — that executing someone for killing another does not bring back the one who is dead, the ones who are dead: for, there is no possibility of balancing the books, and all one is left with is more dead people.

So, an *aporia* — where the sacrality of life is both the limit and condition of both.

Or, if you prefer, an impasse.

Not because either side is wrong — at least not necessarily so — but perhaps, as Albert Camus continues to teach us,[6] « Prometheus is both just and unjust, and Zeus who pitilessly oppresses him also has right on his side. Melodrama could thus be summed up by saying: 'Only one side is just and justifiable', while the perfect tragic formula

---

[6] So, maybe there is *a life after death* — or even (more tantalisingly), *a living which continues after life has ended.*

After all, one can posit that *everyone dies twice*: once bodily, the other time when one has been forgotten. For the luckier among us, it follows that sequence. For the less fortunate, one could well be forgotten before one dies: here, we might even speculate that *being forgotten whilst alive* might well be one definition of *living-dead.*

It also opens the delicious possibility that *reading* is a form of *necromancy.* Which makes the fact that we call attempts to interpret, think, argue, about laws *a reading* rather beautifully-apt, particularly in the context of this meditation: it were always about death.

would be: 'All can be justified, no one is just.' This is why the chorus in classical tragedies generally advises prudence. For the chorus knows that up to a certain limit everyone is right and that the person who, from blindness or passion, oversteps this limit is heading for catastrophe if he persists in his desire to assert a right he thinks he alone possesses ».[7]

But what would *prudence* here mean?

After all, there has been a death — and, quite possibly a senseless one.

One that the law not only has to judge, but — as part of its process — has to also address grievances, mete out punishments, perhaps even attempt to deter future occurrences (even if, perhaps especially if, the latter is an illusion); *en bref*, bring balance back to the system.

All whilst continuing to protect, as it were, the sacredness of life itself.

Which might well be the very problem.

---

[7] Albert Camus, 'On the future of tragedy', translated by Ellen Conroy Kennedy, in *Lyrical and Critical Essays*, edited by Philip Thody. London: Vintage, 1970, 231.

For, if *life is sacred*, it then remains beyond materiality, beyond matter — is abstract.

And it is precisely the focus on the death penalty that allows one to look at life as an idea whilst missing the death around us; to look at the forest and miss the trees, miss the fact that most of the trees might already be missing. This is, for instance, what allows vegans to argue until they are blue in the face about how eating animals violates life whilst ignoring the death of the plants they are consuming.

Where, all that is done is that an *a priori* decision has been made with regard to *what counts as a life*.

Perhaps then, instead of abstracting life, we might attempt to think of the *immanence of the living*. Which means that every living being is unique, singular, aeconomic, non-exchangeable — where each living being is quite possibly unknowable, wholly other from ever other.[8]

---

[8] Which, to be fair, is precisely why pronouncements of guilt are accompanied — framed even (allowing all echoes of accusations, false or otherwise, to resound) — by the phrase, *beyond reasonable doubt*. Innocence is assumed (is axiomatic, and thus always also unattainable; one is, at best, 'not-guilty'); and guilt always only probable: this, in

Which then also opens very uncomfortable, potentially disconcerting, dossiers, notions, questions — such as the fact that every meal is a murder.

Thus, *prudence* is not so much a middle-ground — or, even worse, a moral high ground where one can wash one's hands clean — but the very opposite. It is the concrete place, space, moment in which one bears in mind, along with all the weight that it brings, that *one is only able to live, that one is only living, due to the death of countless others.*

And that one's very responsibility — for, living always already entails responding to and with others, every other, including quite possibly oneself — that one's *being in the world*, hinges around the fact that every moment of living entails, involves, is an act of, choosing who, and what, one kills.

---

recognition of the fact that unknowability remains to haunt all judgments. That even when there is allegedly irrefutable-evidence, one should try not to forget that *forensics* is the *tekhnē* of *prosopopoeia*; that is the craft of making something or someone speak for us, or against another, *as if* they are speaking for themselves. That it is we who be *animating* the knife to speak *as if* it is testifying for or against something; that the so-called smoking gun which seems to be bearing witness to the event remains — and always will be — *utterly and potentially painfully silent*. That its eternal silence quite possibly always and continually haunts, perhaps even judges, any judgment, all decisions, based on it.

Not that we will ever know.

waxing on wagers[9]

THE FLOP

Today, I will explain how the Cabinet reached this decision, and the key considerations that caused us to change our longstanding policy not to allow casinos in Singapore. I also want to acknowledge the concerns of those who oppose or have expressed reservations about an IR, and explain how we propose to limit the negative impact of the casinos. Finally, I hope to bring all Singaporeans together, so that even though we may not all agree on this issue, we understand and respect each other's reasons and concerns, and can close ranks and move ahead.

~ Lee Hsien Loong

In April 2005, then Prime Minister of Singapore, Lee Hsien Loong, raised eyebrows when he announced the advent of casinos — the Marina Bay Sands, and Resort Worlds Sentosa — in Singapore, for it seemed like a sudden shift in state policy.[10] After being resistant to the notion of having casinos on the island for years — according

---

[9] A version of this work was first published as a chapter in *Contemporary Arts as Political Practice in Singapore*, edited by Wernmei Yong Ade & Lim Lee Ching. New York: Palgrave Macmillan, 2016: 13-27.

[10] The casino (or *integrated resort*, if you rather go with the official terminology) in the Marina Bay Sands opened in April 2010, and the corresponding — or competing if you prefer — one at Resort Worlds Sentosa in February 2012.

to Lee's speech, this was hardly the first time the idea had been broached — it seemed like Singapore had made a drastic about-turn. Previous attempts had been turned down due to the perceived social-cost of having a casino on the island. In fact, in a rare move, Lee seemed to seek to appease the populus, or at least address their concerns, by « explaining how the Cabinet reached this decision, and the key considerations that caused us to change our long-standing policy not to allow casinos in Singapore ».[11] In an ever rarer move, he expressedly wanted to « acknowledge the concerns of those who oppose or have expressed reservations about an IR, and explain how we propose to limit the negative impact of the casinos ».[12] However, any illusions about the finality of the state decision were quashed when he uttered, « finally, I hope to bring all Singaporeans together, so that even though we may not all agree on this issue, we understand and respect each other's reasons and concerns, and can *close ranks and move ahead* ».[13]

---

[11] Lee Hsien Loong's speech, entitled 'Proposal to develop Integrated Resorts', was delivered at Parliament House on 18 April, 2005.

[12] *ibid.*

[13] *ibid.* (emphasis mine)

However, this was clearly not an issue of gambling: for, state sponsored gambling — by way of Singapore Pools, « a wholly-owned subsidiary of the Tote Board, established by the Singapore Government in 1968, as Singapore's only legal lottery operator »[14] — has long been a fixture of life in the state. Perhaps then, one can consider if the aversion was not so much to gambling as such but to the notion of a space that was specifically designated for, dedicated to, gambling.

The initial rejection of casinos resulted in much gambling revenue being lost to nearby havens like Genting, Batam, Macau, amongst others: a rather unthinkable decision for a state that prides itself on being the fastest rising economic superpower in South East Asia. To compound matters, the timing of the reversal was rather peculiar: the presence of one casino on the island, let alone two, is no longer a competitive advantage over other states, nations. What was also surprising is the fact that a moral issue — something quite unthinkable in the

---

[14] http://www.singaporepools.com.sg/en/corporate/profile.html, date accessed 28 September 2015.

ultra-pragmatic climate of Singapore[15] — had been seen as a potential stumbling block. One could, however, consider the issue of morality as part of the ruling party's strategy to stay in power: after all, elections still had to be won, and in order to do so, one has to respond, even if, should one be feeling cynical, by way of lip service, to public mores. This attention to the manner in which the casinos would be received can be seen in the fact that in lieu of *casinos*, which were considered a potentially sensitive term, both Marina Bay Sands and Resort Worlds Sentosa are called — named — *integrated resorts*.

---

[15] Opening the register of morality in the issue of casinos is significant in the context of Singapore politics as it is then constituted as a « matter of conscience » ; a situation where the party whip is potentially lifted on the members of the People's Action Party. From 2002, « the whip will be lifted automatically for all MPs on matters of conscience and certain other issues, the party's second Assistant Secretary General, Wong Kan Seng, was reported saying » However, it is not as if there are no limits: « conscience votes will now be allowed on all issues except those affecting the budget, the constitution, no-confidence motions and issues of national security ». (*Agence France Presse*: March 21, 2002).

How « conscience » is separable from any situation involving a judgment and decision is seemingly a separate issue: a sentiment opined by former Nominated MP Siew Kum Hong regarding parliamentary voting over the salaries of cabinet ministers: « it is debatable whether ministerial salaries are a matter of policy or a matter of conscience ». (C.C. Neo. 'Whip to be in place for ministerial salaries debate' in *Today*: 12 January, 2012)

Therefore, one could think of the parliamentary debates over the casinos as either an instance of democracy or a performance of it — not that there is necessarily any difference between the two.

One could, too easily, claim that this term was employed as an attempt to disguise the notion that the casino, rather than being a part of the entire complex, was really its main point. That ultimately, this reversal in policy had nothing to do with social cost. Or, that it was a tacit acknowledgement to the *socius* that it was being *integrated* into the economy; that the lives, and bodies, of people on the island were merely collateral. After all, part of the opposition to the issue had to do with the fact that people felt disempowered, that they perceived that they had no say in their own futures; that everything was laid out for them, to the extent that it felt predetermined.

And the advent of the casinos only exemplified the sentiment that the ruling *nomenklatura* was gambling with the lives, and futures, of its citizens.

This sentiment was exemplified in the protest at Hong Lim Park — when approximately 4000 people gathered on 16 February 2013, to protest the passing of a White Paper in parliament that projected an increase in the island's population to

« between 6.5 to 6.9 million people » by 2030.[16] One could posit that it was not the actual number that incensed the *populus*, but the notion that they had become nothing but numbers. This is exemplified by the fact that one of the most widely circulated photographs of the demonstration, or gathering if you prefer (since permits are required for such events, calling it a protest or a demonstration would be far too ironic), was the sign « Singapore for Singaporeans » ; suggesting that one of the dominant sentiments was a struggle for a certain national identity, for something to identify with.

Just a few months earlier, on the evening of 2 August 2012, Singaporeans were faced with a similar dilemma: should one cheer for Feng Tianwei who had just won an individual bronze medal in table tennis at the London Olympics? After all, this was the first individual Olympics medal that the republic had attained since Tan Howe Liang earned his silver in weightlifting in Rome 52 years before.[17] However, many were still skeptical

---

[16] http://population.sg/whitepaper/resource-files/population-white-paper.pdf

[17] M. Chen, 'Olympics: Feng wins Singapore's 1st individual medal in 52 years' in *Straits Times* (2 August, 2012).

whether Feng — even though she had already been donning state colours for five years; having moved to Singapore under its Foreign Talent Scheme in 2007 and gaining citizenship in January 2008 — was even Singaporean. Naturally, all Singaporeans played along: *we are happy she won, but it would have been so much better if she was actually born here.* And what else is this but protecting the illusion that some actually belong here; are daughters of the land — that even though anyone who bears the right papers, documentation, is technically Singaporean, some have a (greater) right to belong.

For, to utter otherwise would shatter the *omerta*.

It would be to call out that the emperor is naked; that Singapore is nothing other than a name for movement, transit, transaction.

That Feng is precisely a Singaporean as she produces.

Which is why the term 'local talent' is never used: to be considered 'local', one has to always already be a 'talent' — in the specific sense of being productive.

This is exemplified in the seemingly contradictory notion where under Section 377A of the Penal Code[18] homosexual relationships between consenting male adults was punishable by law yet, at the same time, Singapore is one of the gay capitals of Asia. However, this is only paradoxical if one forgets that the notion of *belonging* is intimately tied with production: thus, gay is read as 'happy' as long as one generates; gay is only 'criminally homosexual' if one does not, or even worse, gets in the way of the logic of production.[19]

---

[18] « Any male person who, in public or private, commits, or abets the commission of, or procures or attempts to procure the commission by any male person of, any act of gross indecency with another male person, shall be punished with imprisonment for a term which may extend to 2 years ».

Section 377A of the Penal Code was finally repealed on 29 November 2022.

In what could be read as a bizarre move, Parliament simultaneously endorsed « changes to the Constitution to protect the current definition of marriage from legal challenge », the definition being that of a heterosexual relationship between a 'man' and a 'woman'. (Goh Yan Han, 'Parliament repeals Section 377A, endorses amendments protecting definition of marriage' in *Straits Times*, 29 November 2022).

This manoeuvre is slightly less mad if one reads it as the ruling party responding to its voter-base, which — in its reading — is seen as socially-conservative; and thus the party does not want to be seen as being pro-LGBTQA+.

[19] This could well be also why marriage is defined in that specific manner: for a heterosexual marriage is the only one which potentially produces.

However, harping on the notion of belonging — nationhood even — would be missing the point.

For, what the advent of casinos has revealed is even more terrifying.

For, despite all potential reservations, Singapore is a democracy, is run according to democratic structures — and ultimately, the principle of free elections. And thus, it is precisely the people who are inflicting what they are protesting-against on themselves. For, it is precisely the people that have voted, chosen, cast their lot, for a particular kind of governance; it is them who have determined their own numeralisation, their conversion into numbers, into resources. Thus, unlike other forms of governance — totalitarianism, and fascism, for instance — the *populus* cannot claim that they are coerced, are not able to say that they did not choose whatever is being imposed on them.

For, the rule of democracy is that one accepts the outcome of elections, even if one voted against whomever comes into power.

Hence, casting a vote is placing a bet:[20] regardless of the outcome — and here, it is irrelevant if one actually votes or not; one can always cast an empty bet — the game itself is absolute.

And the convergence of casinos and the White Paper on population has made it all too clear to the *populus* that they are precisely the stake on which this game of numbers is played.

---

[20] Here, we should open our receptors to the echoes of *undi* resounding in the background. In Bahasa Indonesia, it literally means *lot*; where to *berundi* is to *cast one's lot*, both when one gambles, and figuratively when one is *throwing one's lot* behind a certain person, party, politician.

> *The same simplistic and objectivistic misunderstanding occurs with gambling. Here the objective would be economic: to become rich without exerting oneself. The same attempt to skip steps as in magic, The same transgression of the principle of equivalence and hard work which rules the 'real' world. The claim, then, is that gambling's truth is to be found in the tricks it plays on value.*
>
> *But one is forgetting here the game's power of seduction. Not just the power one experiences when momentarily carried away, but the power to transmute values that comes with the rule. In gambling money is seduced, deflected from its truth. Having been cut off from the law of equivalences (it 'burns') and the law of representation, money is no longer a sign or representation once transformed into a stake. And a stake is not something one invests. As an investment money takes the form of capital, but as a stake it appears in the form of a challenge.*
>
> – Jean Baudrillard[21]

But, what precisely is being challenged here?

Which is also the question of *what is at stake?* For, if the state is wagering its *populus* — citizens, if you prefer — then surely the question of *what is it challenging?*, *what is it wagering against?*, comes along with it.

And what else but its very status as a state.

---

[21] Jean Baudrillard, *Seduction*, translated by Brian Singer. Montréal: New World Perspectives — CultureTexts Series, 1990, 139.

For, this is no longer the banal game of politics as form: the game of which party stays in power, of which group of persons manages a population. This is far more serious: this is a state staking on its very status as a state.

Red dot.

The tiny red dot.

The comment that echoes, that stays in the minds of many: the assessment of this island by then Indonesian President Bacharuddin Jusuf Habibie, when he uttered, « it's O.K. with me, but there are 211 million people [in Indonesia]. All the green [area] is Indonesia. And that red dot is Singapore ».[22] Whilst pointing to a map no less. Of course, this was meant as a jibe, a provocation, internal politicking — along with a tad of sabre rattling.

The trouble is: he is right.

But, it is not as if Singapore didn't already know that.

---

[22] R. Borsuk & R. Chua. 'Singapore Strains Relations With Indonesia's President', in *The Asian Wall Street Journal* (4 August 1998).

For, the island has long recognised the folly of the British — they with their notions of Singapore as the *impregnable fortress*. They thought the island was a state. One that could withstand all, hold-off everyone. Now people are making an even greater error (even Habibie who was accidentally right) — they think Singapore is a country.

For, the island is not.

Never was.

Never will be.

The island is a city. More precisely, *a port city*.

Where everyone is welcome; as long as they can « close ranks and move ahead » ; that is, play by the house rules.

Thus, the very trope of Singapore — movement, production, progress — the very cornerstone of its success, is precisely what is effacing its possibility of being a state. And here, one should never forget the echoes of *stasis* in state; the stopping, ceasing, cut-in-motion, needed — even if it is momentary — in order to have any possible notion of itself as a state.

And that is precisely the challenge of the state: wagering that by foregrounding the exchangeability of its populus, the fact that they are only citizens if they are productive, the subjects themselves will raise the stakes — and make meaning where there is none.

THE TURN

She looks like the real thing
She tastes like the real thing
My fake plastic love
But I can't help the feeling
I could blow through the ceiling
If I just turn and run

~ Radiohead[23]

Perhaps this can be our opening gambit: the helplessness that is felt by the protagonist in Radiohead's 'Fake Plastic Trees' is due not so much to the knowledge of her 'fakeness', but that the love for her is felt despite her so-called inauthenticity. And whenever we open the dossier of authenticity, notions of authorship and authority are never far behind. So, as we attempt to explore the vulnerability of the protagonist, we might want to bear in mind — even if this remains a burden on one — the figure of the father, the so-called originator, the one from whom all comes (*auctor*).

And, even if we consider that the love between the protagonist and the « she »

---

[23] Thom Yorke, Johnny Greenwood, Colin Greenwood, Ed O'Brien, and Philip Selway, 'Fake Plastic Trees' in Radiohead, *The Bends*. London: Parlophone Records, 1995.

requires a certain removal of the father — at least a separation — this does not mean that the exorcism is ever fully successful; at the very least, there is no guarantee. This might well be why Prince Hamlet has to momentarily ignore the imperative — plea? — to « remember me » : perhaps only by scribbling it down, jotting down a reminder so that he could return to it later, only by forgetting father, could he go play hooky with Ophelia. Which opens the dossier that it is writing itself that opens the space for the relationship, no matter how momentarily, to play out. Here, one should not forget that in scribbling, there are echoes of *scribere* — tearing. So, even as there might well be shedding of tears, the sweet prince might well be tearing-off a sheet, clearing space, if only for a moment. And as Michel Foucault points out, in a piece he names 'What is an author?' no less, « in writing, the point is not to manifest or exalt the act of writing, nor is it to pin a subject within language; it is, rather, a question of creating a space into which the writing subject constantly disappears ».[24]

---

[24] Michel Foucault, 'What is an author?' in *Language, Counter-Memory, Practice: Selected Essays and Interviews*, translated by Donald F. Bouchard & Sherry Simon. Ithaca: Cornell University Press, 1977, 116.

If daddy refuses to go away,
perhaps I can.

And here, one should try not to forget that it is only memory that keeps one alive. As the protagonist in Edouard Levé's *Suicide* tells us: « you remain alive insofar as those who have known you outlive you. You will die with the last of them. Unless some of them have made you live on in words, in the memory of their children ».[25] But it is not as if one can will forgetting — in fact, by attempting to do so, one only tends to cement the memory; one only continually recalls that one cannot forget, one recalls remembering; one re-members the memory, as it were. Perhaps, it is precisely through scribbling it down, in setting it down — cementing it in words — that Hamlet allows it to temporarily rest. For, here we should not forget: to forget one must lose the object of memory — or, at the very least, its referentiality. The moment the object can be named — the moment there is correspondence between a word and its object — we are back in the provinces of memory. It is only when there is no object —

---

[25] Edouard Levé, *Suicide*, translated by Jan Steyn. Urbana: Dalkey Archive Press, 2008, 6.

or, when the name remains a completely floating signifier[26] — that there can be the possibility of forgetting. In other words, forgetting is the point of full potential; where every possible referent is a possibility. It is the point where one is pre-language; before one is haunted by the spectre of meaning.

Perhaps then, it is by scribbling, writing, that Hamlet sets down the object — frees himself from the very object that lives in memory.

Reciprocity. Where, by letting the object be an object in the fullest sense, an object in full potential, it might leave you alone.

Which might be why, Foucault continues, « writing's relationship with death ... is familiar ».[27] Not just in the senses that he argues for: immortalising through writing (bearing in mind that in order to be immortal one must first pass through death),

---

[26] Here, one could open the dossier of the master-signifier. And, alongside it, the register of whether there is any mastery — any possibility of mastering — a signifier: or, whether it is the signifier that remains master over any signified, any reading, any attempt to signify with it. Perhaps then, forgetting is precisely the impossibility of mastering the master-signifier; or, that the mark of the master-signifier is forgetting; or even, since all we can see is its mark, that the master-signifier is the mark of forgetting.

[27] Michel Foucault, 'What is an author?', 116.

along with the disappearance of the individual that is the writer to become an author. But, that *writing itself* is the very mark of death. For, each time one writes, one has to set down, limit, call forth a capital sentencing on a notion, thought, idea. And that it is only through reading that resurrection occurs. But, even as one can only know one is writing through reading, even as the very witnessing of the inscription is a reading, there is a momentary gap between the death that is written and its resuscitation.

One does not only write death, writing itself is death.[28]

> *And it wears me out,*
> *it wears me out.*

Which might be why writing is always risky. For, if reading is a resurrection, the one who writes has no control over how (s)he is remembered. In writing — in death — the opening of the gap — « creating the space » — for possibility.

---

[28] This notion is explored in greater detail in Jeremy Fernando, *Writing Death*, with a foreword by Avital Ronell. The Hague and Tirana: Uitgeverij, 2011.

One could well accuse Hamlet of shirking responsibility through writing. Of allowing his impulses to take him over, overtake him. Of doing whatever he desired. Of being childish.

Of becoming a child.

But isn't that precisely the point?

And, whenever we speak of body hair, particularly its removal, the dossier of infantilisation is never far behind. It is almost a *de facto* argument within the arsenal of women's studies that accuses systemic patriarchy of reducing the other to the level of the child, the infant, in order to enact a certain control — power — over their bodies.

What is indisputable is the influence of norms. Forming a strict set of rules, one has only one choice: to follow, or not to follow. As Jacques Derrida might say, « you are free, but there are rules ».²⁹ Within the rules one is free to move — but one's movements are already limited; rules form boundaries, and one is very much bound. And, what remains crucial is that even as one has a right to move, one is always already open to inspection, scrutiny, being completely viewed, screened, by the other, by all others: « ... there is a law that assigns the right of inspection, you must observe these rules that in turn keep you under surveillance ».³⁰ And, oftentimes, the other — the *socius*, mores, even the Law — that is doing seeing is one's own self.

Which hardly means that everyone has the same reaction. For, just because those living in the same space — and here, one should open one's receptors to echoes of borders, territories, passports, immigration, amongst other tropes of controlling entrances, maintaining exclusions — are within the same boundaries, does not mean that everyone has the same response, is affected in the same way. As Derrida continues,

---

[29] Jacques Derrida, *Right of Inspection*, translated by David Wills. New York: The Monacelli Press, 1998, 1.

[30] *ibid*, 1.

« anybody ... provided he is skilled at looking, has a right of inspection, which also means the right to interpret whatever is taken into view ». However, one should also recall « we are appropriating this right with an unpardonable violence ».[31] Not just because every interpretive gesture requires a choice, a positing, a taking of a particular position which is always already a part of a certain universal; not just because every appropriation brings with it a propriety over; but also because one can never pardon oneself. Where, it is one — the one who is you — « keeping you under surveillance », in the precise sense of putting the « you » in, within, putting one's own self before the law.

This separation between « you » and one comes about due to the unbridgeable gap that exists within the law itself. As Paul de Man demonstrates, « just as no law can ever be written unless one suspends any consideration of applicability to a particular entity including, of course, oneself, grammatical logic can function only if its referential consequences are disregarded. On the other hand, no law is a law unless it also applies to particular individuals. It

---

[31] *ibid*, 31.

cannot be left hanging in the air, in the abstraction of its generality. Only by thus referring back to particular praxis can the *justice* of the law be tested, exactly as the *justesse* of any statement can only be tested by its referential verifiability, or by deviation from its verification ... ».[32] And the fact that he was meditating upon reading should not be lost upon us: after all, what is the enactment of the law upon oneself but the reading of that law — after which, we write it upon our very selves. The fact de Man is pointing out that reading itself is allegorical might also serve as a warning to us that the object we are approaching — in our attempt to read, even in our best attempts to cautiously, carefully, respectfully, approach it — is always already an object that is being read. After all, « it seems that as soon as a text knows what it states, it can only act deceptively ... and if a text does not act, it cannot state what it knows ».[33] A text always already rests in the gap between — it can only be a text when read, but it needs to be a text to be read. Hence, the text only comes into being through reading, a reading that

---

[32] Paul de Man, *Allegories of Reading: Figural Language in Rousseau, Nietzsche, Rilke, and Proust*. New Haven: Yale University Press, 1979, 268-69.

[33] *ibid*, 270.

can only happen if there is something to be read.

Reading: a non-being, as it were.

Similarly, one should also not forget the fact that norms tend to have arbitrary beginnings. No one is quite sure why body hair should be removed, or not — where should it be maintained, and where not. However, in just about every culture, there is a rule.

And, in many ways, it is precisely the arbitrariness of it that remains interesting.

Based on nothing.

Authored into being.

For, one has to remember that authority cannot be demanded, nor imposed: it must be granted onto one by another, by others. In fact, authority cannot even be demonstrated, performed. For, as Avital Ronell teaches us, the moment authority shows itself it loses all authority: this is due to the fact that « authority does not belong to the class of action or syntax of being that can be 'exercised', that is, in any significant way flexed, handled ».[34] Thus, even as it is related to power, authority must not, can never, utilise power.

In other words, authority is always already only *in potential*.

Which might be why there is always so much anxiety, particularly amongst incumbent parties, whenever there is a general election. And there is perhaps nowhere that it was more obvious in Singapore than during the run up to the 2015 General Election: when, even though, perhaps especially since, there was no actual chance (nor even a remote possibility) the People's Action Party was ever going to lose its ruling majority. Their anxiousness — real or performative — could be felt most in statements warning people of the « severe, if not tragic, consequences » of a *wrong* decision. Rifting on the economic register that resounds with the electorate, then PAP Chairman, Khaw Boon Wan, added, « we all do such due diligence when we want to buy a new apartment ... GE is even more important than buying an apartment ». And

---

[34] Avital Ronell, *Loser Sons: Politics and Authority*. Illinois: University of Illinois Press, 2012, 21.

for his *coup de grace*, Khaw proclaimed — without a trace of irony — « we cannot be sure of a PAP government on Sept 12 »[35] ; somewhat missing the point of an election. Whilst one might chuckle, perhaps even mock, the nervousness of the ruling party — or, if one is feeling more cynical, deride the blatant emotional politicking — one must also bear in mind that each time there are elections, one can also hear echoes of daddy pleading to be remembered: not just in the sense of *please do not forget me* but, more pertinently, cries of *return me to power*, *re-member* me, *re-authorise* me.

For, with every tick in the ballot box, at the cast of each lot — the moment of the *undi*, as it were — each person is quite literally writing authority into being.

In the same vein, one can never confer upon oneself the title author. One can only write; it is only when the work written is seen, recognised, by others that one potentially becomes an author. More precisely, at the point one is seen to have a certain authority over that particular work.

---

[35] S. Khalik & Y-C. Tham, 'No guarantee that PAP will be in government after polls: Khaw Boon Wan' in *The Straits Times* (8 September, 2015).

Perhaps the question should not just be 'what is an author?', but also *who authorised the author?*

Or even, *who authors the author?*

And if we open the register that the removal of body hair is a kind of authoring, a writing onto oneself, to how one is seen, the dossier of a writing that removes, a writing that erases, has to also be attended to.

This is *a writing of disappearance* — where what is removed does not leave one denuded, open, but rather veils. For, we must never forget that as much as this is an erasure, this erasing also writes the *socius* onto our bodies.

A writing that writes as it erases.

Thus, not just a removal.

But, always already, a sculpting.

And here, we should open our receptors to echoes of sugaring from Ancient Egypt that resound in contemporary practices of waxing; keeping in mind the fact that all Egyptian divinities are depicted completely hairless. A gesture perhaps to the divine but, more importantly, that our only link to the divine is through a ritual. Which is not to suggest that to wax is to attempt to become, or to be closer, to the gods (that would be too banal), but that waxing itself is the ritual.

A wager, if you will.

Which opens the question: what is at stake in this wager?

And what else but the self.

Not in the banal sense of: *this is who I am* — a pitiful kind of identity politics — but a far more profound one; an attempt to disappear.

An attempt to become an object.

For, we should not forget that in many ways it is precisely hair patterns — even and perhaps especially when it comes to body hair — that sets us apart. This is why barbers, salons, hair-stylists, waxing studios, pubic styles, hair styles, have become such a significant part of staking our claim on individuality — an attempt at differentiating ourselves from another, any other, every other. Even to the paradoxical extent of buying into trends, movements, fashions (for instance, the absurdity of the hippie movement and its claim of finding oneself, being yourself, whilst being a collective movement). What else could this be but an attempt to discover oneself by making oneself exactly the same as every other — an effacement of every difference in order to assert the notion that difference is the starting point.

Or, as our Thai friends might say: we are *same same but different.*

And here, we should remember that this phrase is most often used, heard, when one has just accused a shopkeeper of selling exactly the same item for a higher price; that is, when there is absolutely no material difference. The difference that the shopkeeper is referring to is neither metaphysical nor about the singularity of the context (for even though those are possibilities, neither would make sense in relation to a situation when both parties are haggling over prices) but is a performative statement; which translates to: *there are differences because it is different.* That is: *it is different as such*; and there is no referentiality to this difference.

Which means: *the singularity of each piece — each person — is exemplified precisely because there are innumerable others exactly like it ... just elsewhere.*

Perhaps then, not a surprise — allowing all echoes of excess, abundance, *sur-*, to resound here — that the proliferation of waxing studios in Singapore comes alongside the advent of casinos.

The wager here: in the excess of the same, one might catch a glimpse of the possibility of the singular.

And if I could be who you wanted
If I could be who you wanted, all the time

~ Radiohead

And how else to be the *who you wanted, all the time* of the protagonist Thom Yorke sings about except by being, becoming, anything — *any thing* — you wanted.

Keeping in mind Jean Baudrillard's reminder that, « the great stars or seductresses never dazzle because of their talent or intelligence, but because of their absence. They are dazzling in their nullity ... ».[36]

By being — perhaps, even becoming — an object.

Not just any object; but one that remains enigmatic.

For, if too familiar, if already in the family — where one can recognise precisely where it is from, where the mark of daddy is too clear — there is no longer any mystery. However, if too strange, overly other, it would also be unapproachable.

Thus, an object that is *strangely familiar*; uncanny.

Same same but different.

---

[36] Jean Baudrillard. *Seduction*, translated by Brian Singer. Montréal: New World Perspectives — CultureTexts Series, 1990, 96.

THE RIVER

The beloved
is a sensuous object.

~ Friedrich Engels & Karl Marx[37]

> *If production can only produce objects or real*
> *signs, and thereby obtain some power; seduction,*
> *by producing only illusions, obtains all powers,*
> *including the power to return production and*
> *reality to their fundamental illusion.*
>
> ~ Jean Baudrillard[38]

If the casinos reveal too much, too clearly, perhaps then waxing — concealing by denuding, hiding through a surplus of revelation — is what maintains the illusion of the subject.

Waxing as a wager to take on another wager; where the individual thrusts herself (after all, it is the feminine that has always been transgressive, the masculine caught up in power has always been doomed from the

---

[37] Friedrich Engels & Karl Marx, *The Holy Family or Critique of Critical Criticism: Against Bruno Bauer and Company*, translated by Richard Dixon. Moscow: Foreign Languages Publishing House, 1956, 18.

[38] Jean Baudrillard, *Seduction*, 70.

beginning) into the game of becoming an object — a number amongst numbers.

Taking the game itself to its extremes, as it were.

Taking precisely the logic of casinos, where numbers themselves are the stake, to its very limits.

Which brings us back to the raising of stakes we were first speaking of: that of the subject and meaning; in particular, the subject making meaning where there is none. Not by attempting to author a meaning, by writing this meaning onto herself — that would be far too obvious a manoeuvre; and here, one must never forget that it is a game of one-upmanship — but precisely by disappearing. This is gambling not just in the sense of *you got to know when to hold 'em, know when to fold 'em* — as Kenny Rogers might say — but, more radically, that one has to disappear into the game itself: where one's opponent no longer even realises that they are in a duel, for the duality has seemingly vanished.

I will no longer be your mirror!

For, the wager of the state be that the *populus* would attempt to reinscribe themselves into the state by giving some meaning, whatever meaning, to being Singaporean. That the people would not have been able to cope with the purely transitory, pure movement, of the port: and by foregrounding it through the advent of casinos, the people would subjectify themselves in order to belong.

The fact that Singaporeans had to pay $100 (now $150) to enter the casinos would be testament to this strategy: it is not just that one has to pay to enter; it is that *one has to buy-in to belong*.

And, it is not as if this wager is ineffective.

For, one should not forget that much of the population seems to have decided to play this game: one only has to witness the growing xenophobia in the state — the discomfort with foreigners; the typical criticism that those who come to the island have to fit in; the accusation of the dilution of Singaporean culture (whatever that even means) — to sense this.

However, there is also the possibility — and one must not give up on this — that the proclamation « Singapore for Singaporeans » is completely ironic. That the tautological structure of the phrase is precisely an attempt to render it meaningless: phatic communication at its best.

A cry of indignation: bringing with it echoes of, « if you do not let us dream we will not let you sleep ».[39]

A cry that does not ask for anything in particular but is, instead, a challenge to the system: for the state to maintain itself as state, by making meaning where there is none. After all, one should never forget that cries (*les cris*) potentially always also write (*écrit*) onto us.

Thus, quite literally — an attempt to *wax lyrical*.

Keeping in mind that in its incarnation as a verb, it does the very opposite of ripping out, exfoliate; is instead a growth, an augmenting.

---

[39] An echo of the *Los Indignatos* slogan: « *si no nos dejáis soñar, no os dejaremos dormir* ».

And this is perhaps the very wager of the one who waxes: that by making oneself an object, one seduces the state into writing a subject — its own subjectification — into being.

Which would, ironically, be democracy in its purest sense: where the *demos* — the *populus* — are the ones who truly wield the power.

It might well be that one cannot quite justify this claim, legitimise it, let alone prove it.

But, perhaps here, one could take a page from Hélène Cixous and her reimagining of Medusa. And take seriously the ironic claim of Paul Virilio: *all power to the imagination.*

For, imagination is not of the order of power: if it were, it would merely be back in the same discourse, attempting to do precisely what power does — influence — merely reinforce the same game. Power trembles at imagination precisely because it is not the same; similar enough to lure, seduce, power into its game, but not the same — it is *same same but different*. For, imagination opens a gap for power to jump into — and by doing so, power undoes itself. Precisely by allowing it a space to read itself — potentially re-write itself — ; giving it enough rope to hang itself.

A waxing during which one does not scream; even when one's roots are being forcibly ripped-out.

But, a waxing that never forgets the echoes of *radical* in roots.

Where the one being waxed chuckles; and why not — laughs.

And by doing so, unsettles.

For, there is no challenge like laughter: not only does it come from elsewhere, not only does it sometimes take over one's self, it also potentially spreads, affects, infects. Not by trying to affect — this is not power — but by opening one, perhaps only momentarily, to the absurdity of a situation. At the end of which — when laughter ceases — the source and reason for its outbreak remain a mystery, beyond comprehension, reason.

Never forgetting that in every ceasing, there are echoes of a cut, a wounding, puncture, opening, *caesura*.

Quite possibly, a ruptured *stasis* — a shattered state.

And at this, power trembles.

This, is our wager.

on leaders;
or, Splinter taught them to be ...[40]

> *Dancing with the devil.*
> *Call it respect,*
> *Call it fear.*
>
> ~ Stevie Nicks[41]

As the world increasingly comes to terms with accusations of betrayals, of collusions with oppressive regimes — from dalliances with dictators, to the selling-out of public institutions to corporations who are hell-bent on profiteering from every aspect of our lives, corporeal or virtual — what has been constantly, and repeatedly (*ad nauseum*), brought to the fore is the question of the relationship between leaders of a country and those who vote them into power.

Which begs the Question: *what does it mean to lead* alongside *what does it mean to be a leader?* The critique that is loudest is that leaders abuse their positions as leaders. That even though they are in a position to direct, even

---

[40] A version of this work was first published as 'An essay on what it is to be a leader' in *VICE UK*, on 3 April, 2013.

[41] Stevie Nicks, Dave Grohl, and Taylor Hawkins, 'You Can't Fix This' in *Sound City: Real to Reel* (soundtrack). New York: RCA Records, 2013.

though they are put in positions that could readily benefit themselves, they should know better.

Which translates to: being a leader means that one is above mere feelings.

There is, of course, nothing new in this criticism: each time a person in public office falls from grace, what they are accused of is falling prey to their own desires as humans; a regression from one who adopts a particular position, role, to merely being a person.

For instance, even after the alleged evidence against Andrew Mitchell was called into question, the mere fact that he might have uttered the word « plebs » — or even better, looked like the kind of person that would have said it — is held against him: his resignation amidst the media furore, regardless of the facts, would suggest this. The fact that everybody also missed the point that Mitchell refused a lawful instruction — to use a different gate — should not be lost on us: for, this suggests that this is no longer a case where what actually happened matters any longer. What seems to be at stake is whether a leader is able to separate the position from the self: in other words, if one is a leader, one has to be other from one's self. In Mitchell's case, regardless of how he felt — after all, one would be hard pressed to completely disagree with his case that the police should be there to assist rather than deter his movements — he should have been able to bottle it up, and say only what his public position would.

Thus, a good leader is one who is able to divorce their selves from their role: upon assuming their mantle as leader, they should be able to become non-human.

Whether this is realistic or not is beside the point: the fact that the public continues to be shocked each time it happens suggests it be a fantasy that is expected to be maintained. In his piece, '*Plebgate* was never about Tory toffs', Geoffrey Wheatcroft argues that the incident captured our attention as it « revealed our prejudices » ; in particular that « a deplorable number of people — including journalists, who are meant to be natural sceptics — had been ready to believe a patently implausible story, because Mitchell is a well-heeled, expensively educated Tory, and because 'it was the kind

of thing he would have said' ».⁴²
Unfortunately Wheatcroft's ending — « after decades of fawning on the police and truckling to the federation, our politicians might finally take a stand, and take them on » — his call to arms, as it were, equally misses the point. For, what was at stake here were « prejudices » and the police, just not in the way he claims: rather, it is our policing of prejudices — the lengths to which we would go to protect the illusions that govern our lives, up to believing the very people we would never trust in the first place, the police — that is revealed here.

Here, the irony that in an alleged democracy the private sphere is expected to be subsumed under the public — the very hallmark of fascism—should not be lost on us.

And as we have learned from Stalin, the moment appearances are ruptured, reality itself collapses: for, it is not just that one has to agree with Stalin all the time, one also has to maintain the illusion that free discourse is possible; otherwise the fantasy that Stalin

---

[42] Geoffrey Wheatcroft. '"Plebgate" was never a story about Tory toffs'. *The Guardian* (3 February, 2013)

has been freely chosen to lead the people, that he is the first servant as it were, is destroyed.

And the whole game comes crumbling down.

Perhaps this is why the public is harshest on the ones who call themselves 'public servants': their fall from grace only serves to remind everyone else that *if the alleged best that was on offer is that bad, what more everyone else; and even worse, what more ourselves.* This might well be why Silvio Berlusconi's *non sequitur* of a defense — « *Io non sono un santo* »[43] — rankles everyone so badly. Not because it isn't true, but because he is being absolutely honest. And it is this brutal candidness that ruptures our illusions.

The importance of keeping up appearances is appreciated fully by the incumbent party in Singapore: which is why any party member who is deemed to have transgressed (no matter how irrelevant the transgression in relation to and with either

---

[43] « There are tons of good-looking girls and entrepreneurs out there ... I am not a saint ... »

Silvia Aloisi, '"I'm no saint," Berlusconi says after sex tapes' in *Reuters* (22 July, 2009):

the job-scope or their role as a politician) is made to resign. This is seen most recently in a scandal involving then Speaker of Parliament, Tan Chuan-Jin. After having been outed as having an « inappropriate relationship » by way of an extra-marital affair, Tan resigned from his roles as Speaker, Member of Parliament, all of his public roles, and his party-membership; even though the affair had naught to do with his actual roles nor his abilities to perform them.[44] Tan's resignation echoes with the resignation of the previous-but-one Speaker, Michael Palmer, who was also compelled to leave his post after admitting to an extra-marital affair. In his resignation, Palmer refers to the affair as a « grave mistake » ; highlighting the fact that the gravity lies not so much in one's ability to do a job but in how one is perceived. In fact, one could even argue that the ability to do the job is almost less important than maintaining the image of spotlessness, faultlessness.[45] One could also open the register that Palmer had recognised that it is

---

[44] Ang Hwee Min, 'Tan Chuan-Jin, Cheng Li Hui continued 'inappropriate relationship' even after being told to stop: PM Lee' in *Channel News Asia* (17 July 2023).

[45] 'Speaker of Parliament Michael Palmer resigns over "grave mistake"' in *Channel News Asia* (12 December, 2012).

impossible to divorce the person from the position; not just in the sense that the position maketh the man, but that the person, the self, infects the position itself.

Where, the illusion that a leader is non-human must be maintained; particularly in a technocratic society where everything running like clockwork, as a machine, is the fantasy.

But one never allowed the devil
to come to the party

~ Stevie Nicks

Which brings us back to the very beginning, to the point at which we began; in particular, to accusations of collusion, collaboration, with regimes and organisations usually considered beyond the pale. For, it is not as if accusations of these kinds are anything new: no one seems to mind the fact that to win the Second World War the alliance happily included Stalin, one of the most notorious mass murderers of all time. Which is not to say that the number of people murdered should be any basis of judgement

— that would not only be banal, but utterly obscene; as if one could equate, calculate, measure, lives, life.

But the question remains: *why is it that associations, dalliances, with particular kinds of leaders raises the ire of the public more than others?*

Perhaps it is the fact that some leaders — Muammar Gaddafi, the trio-of-Kims, Vladimir Putin, Alexander Lukashenko, Hun Sen, Ne Win, (insert your favourite dictator) — expose, unveil, the illusion of *the leader* more than others; in particular, the notion of a leader — the notion of the one who shows the way — being the very illusion that must be preserved.

And here, we must not forget that the leader is the one who guides (*agogos*) — and thus, the very action, body, of the leader is what matters.

This might well be why the figure of the one who is sure, is certain, who commands respect, is the archetypal leader — which is why Winston Churchill still holds a place in the hearts of many; the leader is not so much a person of thought, consideration —

least of all doubt — but a person of action, one who does (even if this entails genocide).

But it is not as if this ceasing of thought — in order to act, to decide, one has to enact, if only momentarily, a cut, a caesura, on thinking — can spill over too far, into utter thoughtlessness. If that were the case, Bush Jr. and Donald Trump would have been the poster boys for leadership.[46]

Thus, what a leader has to do, in order to be recognised as a leader — and this is where we should take the notion of *figure* (where one can slide meaning into, impose oneself onto) seriously — is to demonstrate *performativity of thought whilst acting*. Which might well be why holding one's chin whilst pointing in some general direction is one of the classic poses of 'leadership'.

However, by taking it one step too far, by making it too-obvious that one is making a performance out of leadership, one can also rupture the illusion of disinterestedness — distance, gap, between the self and the

---

[46] Which is not to say both of them don't have their respective fan clubs; of course they do — particularly the latter — but so does everyone. It would also be a stretch of the imagination to say that either of them (in spite of the latter's delusions) would be the Pictionary entry for this.

position — that leadership, or more precisely, this figure, requires. We find this exemplified in Gaddafi and his 'Amazonian Guards': it is not so much the fact that he surrounded himself with beautiful women that was the issue,[47] but that he was clearly enjoying the attention he received with, and through, this procession. And perhaps even: enjoying it too-much, to the point that he almost seemed to be taking the piss (it's no wonder Hilary Clinton and Barack Obama seemed all too ready to engineer his downfall: the gall of Gaddafi having fun with his security detail whilst they had to endure the drudgery of the Secret Service).[48] And while we are thinking of Gaddafi, we should not forget the accompanying echoes of Berlusconi each time the Libyan dictator is mentioned: need anyone say *bunga bunga party*?

---

[47] Despite what contemporary leaders like to say — especially those who like to appear to be 'with the times' — leadership and inclusivity, equality of power, non-hierarchies, and such things, are anathema to each other. In many ways, such utterances might well be instances of leaders precisely demonstrating a performativity of thought — by way of self-reflexivity — while acting.

[48] This being the reason behind the fixation on Bill Clinton and his blowjob in the Oval Office: his « grave mistake » was in not-appearing *grave enough*.

And this brings about the opposite effect of Han Christian Andersen's warning in *The Emperor's New Clothes*: for here, it is not so much that a child might be able to shatter the illusion and thus had to be told to shut up but a much worse situation: the illusion itself has already been shattered, and it is us that be holding it together.

·

All transgressions are possible,
but not the infraction of the rule.

~ Jean Baudrillard[49]

And what is this rule that has been *infracted*, that has been fractured, ruptured?: what else but the fantasy that it is the leader that leads. For, if what has been foregrounded is the fact that it is the *people* who are propping up not just the leader (everyone already knows that) but the very notion of the leader itself — the very *figure* of the leader — then reality itself crumbles.

This was the lesson lying within the London School of Economics' dalliance with the

---

[49] Jean Baudrillard, *Seduction*, translated by Brian Singer. Montréal: New World Perspectives — CultureText Series, 1990, 126.

Gaddafis: it is not so much that universities have been accepting money from questionable sources; it is even less so that universities are now full-on card-carrying corporations, mere business entities; but it is that by awarding Saif al-Islam Gaddafi his doctorate whilst simultaneously accepting donations from the NGO Gaddafi Foundation, LSE has shattered all illusions of meritocracy. This is why the pariahs of academia are 'degree mills': it is not so much that universities do not sell degrees (try not paying your fees), but that we need to maintain the possibility that we have actually earned them with our intellectual ability.

And what else maintains the possibility more than the space of metaphor — the figure — itself.

For, we should try not to forget the fact that figures work precisely because they give us the room to insert our own meaning, our own possibilities, within them. By collapsing the person and the position — by demonstrating all too clearly the human — Gaddafi, Berlusconi, Palmer, Mitchell, Tan, and countless others, have foregrounded Italo Calvino's lesson from 'A King Listens':

that anyone can be King, as long as (s)he wields the sceptre and crown.[50]

And this is what truly scares us: not just that the leader that we are following, that we in fact are holding up, might have been us (with all our failings; faults that are too apparent to us), but that the leader is us.

Not in a mystical mumbo-jumbo sense of we are all one body (despite what the fascists would like to believe), but in an even more radical sense: that we have imbued the leader, the one we follow, with our fantasies of what it is to be a leader.

The leader: the one who leads.

And us: who are led.

Always already in a relationship with each other: but with a space, a gap; otherwise the leader and the ones led would be the same. This being precisely the space of the figure.

---

[50] Italo Calvino, 'A King Listens' in *Under the Jaguar Sun*, translated by William Weaver. London: Vintage, 1993.

Which is why Hugo Chavez's body will be put on permanent display.[51] Not so much to remember his life, but as a reminder that he — like Lenin, Mao Zedong, Ho Chi Minh, Kim Il-Sung, Kim Jong-Il, et al — is dead. Which is not to say that the body of Chavez would have no effect; of course it would. But, that it would affect us precisely by being an object — static, decorative, practically an accessory, certainly a sight for tourists; and, most importantly, meaningless (in the precise sense of: *I can be whatever you want me to be*).

---

[51] 'Hugo Chavez's body to be put on permanent display' in *Today* (8 March, 2013).

Most things, alas, have meaning and depth;
but only some of them rise to the level of appearances,
and they alone are truly seductive ...

~ Jean Baudrillard[52]

·

Which opens a new reading to the oft-used phrase, *lead by example*. For, it is not so much what a leader does — echoes here of *do as I say not as I do* resound — but that it be the appearance of being a leader, maintaining the figure of a leader, that is crucial. Not that there is a definite, nor definable notion of what a leader is: but that is the point.

It is by being whatever you want them to be that they lead.

And if you are asking the question, *is the man walking the dog or is the dog walking the man?*, you are missing the point. What matters is the leash; the relation between the dog and the man, the leader and the one is being led.

---

[52] Jean Baudrillard, *Seduction*, 117.

After which, both the dog and the man can play their respective roles.

I place some flowers, orange and blue, upon your grave[53]

Many moons ago, while learning about the process of making paper in the basement workshops of the Singapore Tyler Print Institute, master paper-maker Gordon Koh, in the midst of handing around a sheet for us to look at to feel, turned to me and uttered, « paper has a good memory ».

By this he meant, paper takes on what has last *touched* it before *becoming* paper.[54]

It is, thus, no wonder that alumni, students, and faculty, both current and former, of Yale-NUS College, particularly those who were part of, have a connection-with, *felt for*, the arts and humanities, have chosen to

---

[53] The subtitle to this piece should really be 'on mournings, memories, remembrances, and the curious case of the arts & humanities at Yale-NUS College': such subterranean shenanigans might be most apt found playing footsie in a footnote.

[54] Perhaps *becoming* always entails *being moved by* what touches one. How fetching!

Whether volition is involved is quite another question: not all touchings are called for, wanted, sought out; even those which might shape us, perhaps even most benefit us (the *you asked for it* just before getting smacked opens the possibilities that either the *you* who called for it has very little to do with the *I* who is about to receive, or that sometimes we don't even know what we want; the two not being mutually exclusive).

commit their memories of the college — of their time in and with the space; by making and remaking works that have shaped and perhaps will continue to mold what has become the worlds of the place — onto paper, into an anthology they have named *Magic|Unfold*.⁵⁵

A title without articles no less: for magic not only unfolds its own time, but *is* its own time.

---

⁵⁵ *Naming things is never innocent. It is to precipitate them beyond their own existence into the ecstasy of language which is already the ecstasy of their end.*

~ Jean Baudrillard

And like all *cool memories*, they perhaps have to be set aside, even hidden away, in a footnote. Lest they become *hot*.

Something co-editor, artist and professor, Yanyun Chen,[56] reminds us during the book launch and accompanying exhibition on a balmy — one is tempted to say it involved thunder, lighting, rain (for there were certainly stirrings in the air) — for the moment[57] let's stay with tropical Saturday evening: « you all will write the legend of this place. »[58]

In time.

Whomever you are. And, *will become.*

Dengan ramuan-ramuan sendiri.

---

[56] Dr Chen is a visual artist who was a lecturer in the Division of Arts & Humanities at Yale-NUS College from August 2015 to July 2023. She is the editor of the *Magic*.

[57] Perhaps already a reason not to trust writers.

> *I say this to whoever wants to listen: when we believe we see the life and work fusing in the figure of a writer, let us consider that their life is deliberately false and has been invented solely to support the work, which truly is real.*
>
> ~ Enrique Vila-Matas

[58] As part of her speech at the launch of the anthology at Yale-NUS College on Saturday, 18 January 2025, which was accompanied an art exhibition — featuring 39 works by students, alumni, faculty, former faculty, and guests artists — named *Magic Hour*, curated by Julianne Thompson, Tay Ying, and Christophe Draeger.

> *When the bricks finally fall, and the name eventually disappears, and the tides retrieve these remnants back into an ocean of time, it is the people who will write it back into a glittering existence. Except, this time, there are no rules to hold us back. Afterall, legends are crafted with magic.*
>
> ~ Yanyun Chen[59]

So not just that the event was a magical hour — of readings, speeches, presentations, laughter, reminiscings — even as the gathering could well be read as a memorial, as eulogies to invoke, resurrect, revive, summon, conjure, memories of « an Arts & Humanities major in the sole liberal arts college in Singapore »[60] ; *mourning* can also be magical. Nor just that each time you open the two books, one can also be plunged back into those times; *remembering* is another form it can take. But that any hour can be magic.

For, as Michel Deguy continues to teach us, « poetry is not about seeing the invisible, nor the very visible. Poetry, instead, is about

---

[59] Yanyun Chen, 'Ramuan' in *Magic: Art Practices at Yale-NUS College*, 6.

[60] *ibid*, 5.

seeing the slightly visible ».⁶¹ What was always there, in front of us, if we learn to see, hear, listen.

If we take the time to do so.

If we give our time to do so.

If you give yourself the gift of time to do so.⁶²

> *If a poem is a kind of folding in of both sense and sentiment, let your reading of this anthology be the forever unfolding of what is yet to come.*
>
> ~ Lawrence Lacambra Ypil⁶³

•

---

[61] This was Michel Deguy's beautiful response to my question, « what, to you, is poetry? », which I posed to him at the end of Judith Balso's seminar, *Poetry & Philosophy* — at which he was the guest poet — at The European Graduate School in August 2004.

[62] Whilst bearing in mind that every gift can always also be *giften* ... if only to yourself. Be careful what you wish for. Or summon.

[63] Lawrence Lacambra Ypil, 'Preface: Sentiment and Sense' in *Unfold: Creative Writing at Yale-NUS College*, 5.

Lawrence Lacambra Ypil is a Senior Lecturer of Creative Writing, and the coordinator of the Creative Writing Track in the Division of Arts and Humanities, at Yale-NUS. He is the co-editor of *Unfold*, alongside Lishani Ramanayake, Shawn Hoo, and Myle Yan Tay.

A book is a huge cemetery in which on the majority of the tombs the names are effaced and can no longer be read.

~ Marcel Proust[64]

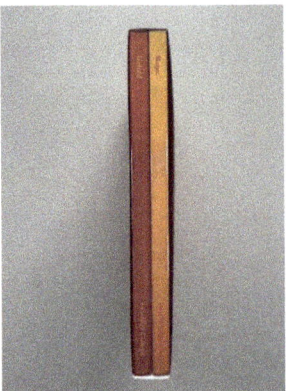

So what then do we make of these two tomes?

Aside each other |

Like lovers.

---

[64] Marcel Proust, *Time Regained*, vol. 6 of *In Search of Lost Time*, translated by Andreas Mayor and Terence Kilmartin. New York: Random House, 1993, 310.

After all, it is not as if visual arts and creative writing don't go hand-in-hand. Gallivanting by the oculus. Incestuous cousins.

One might also see this as two tombs — each with, in, within, their own world — facing each other. Two languages, almost adversarial; never the twain shall meet, in their absolute un-translatability.

> *When you finish anything, people want you to then talk about it. And I think it's almost like a crime. A film or a painting – each thing is its own sort of language and it's not right to try to say the same thing in words. The words are not there. The language of film, cinema, is the language it was put into, and the English language — it's not going to translate. It's going to lose.*
>
> *~ David Lynch*[65]

Held together only by the outer casing, casket, binding them together, their wills be damned. But, perhaps only flimsily.

Much like how the hyphen in the name of the college brings together yet forever keeps asunder.

---

[65] Roy Caroll, 'David Lynch: You gotta be selfish. It's a terrible thing' in *The Guardian*, 23 June 2018.

With urgency, fighting against erasure and forgetting, we — editors, curators, artists, writers, administrators, students, alumni, and faculty — have gathered to imagine an anthology, offering shelter to more than a decade's worth of creative work made under the shade of the Arts & Humanities at Yale-NUS College.

~ Yanyun Chen[66]

Matter. Materials.

The activity of working, erasing and further reworking of materials is understood not as an imposition of theme, form or meaning, but as movement through matter.

~ Vince Briffa[67]

Of what matters.

---

[66] Yanyun Chen, 'Ramuan', 5.

[67] In conversation with Vince Briffa about his artistic process after my performance-lecture — 'On writing — writhing, crying, screaming', featuring the charcoal sketches of Yanyun Chen — at The University of Malta on 24 March, 2016.

Yet, the thing about grasping at grief is that the more you squeeze, the more sand trickles through your fingers

~ Yanyun Chen[68]

To whom it may concern.

Well you can bump and grind
It is good for your mind
Well you can twist and shout
Let it all hang out
But you won't fool the children of the revolution
No, you won't fool the children of the revolution
No, no, no

~ T-Rex[69]

« With urgency, fighting against ... »

---

[68] Yanyun Chen, 'Ramuan', 5

Chen continues: « What does one choose to remember, choose to write down, choose to mark onto a surface that could somehow, no matter how imperfectly, capture years of conversations, friendships, artistic efforts, grime in the sink, paint stains on the floor, scribbles on crumpled sheets of paper, deleted files, and wet tissues? Whose memories get to remain, and whose left out? And, why? »

After all, as Max Porter so beautifully, devastatingly, reminds us, « grief is the thing with feathers ».

[69] Marc Bolan, 'Children of the Revolution', single. London: EMI Records, 1972.

« No, no, no »

For, freedom comes with the ability to say « no » ; and more than just a denial, a « no » that can be uttered without negating the one who speaks, without effacing oneself. This, after all, be one of the cornerstone of *dialektikē*; Pericles would almost certainly agree.⁷⁰

Bearing in mind, even if this remains a burden on one (no one ever said all memories are pleasant), this « no » is always also in response to something, that one is « fighting against », some things, some one(s), others, orders.

For, *to revolt* entails first being revolted by.

---

[70] It is probably no coincidence or a perfect confluence — whichever version of magic you prefer — that the Founding President of Yale-NUS College would be likewise named. Magic unfolds in its own time.

> *What you leave behind is not engraved in stone monuments, but what is woven into the lives of others.*
>
> ~ Pericles*

*No written works of Pericles have survived so you'll just have to take my word for it. Ah, magic (trickery).

And make no mistake there was here a revolution taking place — by « gather[ing] to imagine ».[71]

But not one which involves merely going around in circles; a carnivalesque release in order that the day after be a return to 'business as usual', to order. *Imagination*, instead, entails « opening a new world in an old world », as Alain Badiou would say,[72] a world of commons, community, a *we* who had been part of Yale-NUS College, from the point of view of the *us*, an experience which was shared and which has now shaped,

---

[71] Particularly pertinent in a state where a *gathering of one* can be defined as an *illegal assembly*. Perhaps Singapore has always been better readers of Deleuze and Guattari than we imagined.

> *Just because you do not take an interest in politics doesn't mean politics won't take an interest in you.*
>
> ~ Pericles

And yes, if you listened carefully, it would not have been difficult to hear John Lennon humming in the background.

[72] « Opening a new world in an old word » being one of Badiou's definition of an event. So not a founding of some fabled, imaginary, other world, separate from the one in which we are living — as found in so many utopian or dystopian world-views (hello Elon), transcendental philosophies, and religions — but as a rupture in the old world which opens possibilities that were always inherent, there, not just unrealised, but unnoticed.

To read more, please see Alain Badiou, *Being and Event*, translated by Oliver Feltham. London: Continuum, 2006.

formed, informed, reformed, deformed, us in our own singular ways.

Our own singular ways: therefore always already multiple. A *we* that is not monolithic, uniform, same, but a community that comes together in its plurality, where what is common is our very differences.

An *inoperative community* if you prefer ... that cannot be co-opted, nor spoken for; nor where anyone can speak-for, claim to represent, any other, let alone all others.

You may say I'm a dreamer
But I'm not the only one

~ John Lennon[73]

Which is not to say there be no risks involved. For to revolt, one has to also open one's self to voltages, to being struck, to electric shocks even. Perhaps turning us into — if we are not already — Frankenstein's monsters.

---

[73] John Lennon & Yoko Ono, 'Imagine' in John Lennon, *Imagine*. London: Apple Records, 1971.

Certainly gadflies.

Which, as should have come as no surprise to anyone; for the college — particularly the Division of Arts & Humanities — has always been seen to be, been certainly treated as, an irritant to be at-best-tolerated, ideally swatted-aside, even better if squashed, by the powers-that-be.

But I suppose, there are also some benefits to being treated like shit. That is, after all, where the most beautiful of flowers bloom.

Even if you're betrayed, continue to trust humankind.

~ Hélène de Beauvoir[74]

Eventually to-become a gathering (*logia*) of flowers (*anther*).

Their very own 花樣年華.

Oh there is always love involved.

And this is certainly a mood.

---

[74] Amy Fleming, "Jean-Paul Sartre hid at her house!' The forgotten brilliance of Hélène de Beauvoir, sister of Simone' in *The Guardian*, 20 January 2025.

And should anyone accuse this as being a slinking-off into a corner, a backing-off into the shadows, of taking shelter between the covers of a book (after all, who even reads anymore!), even a flight into script, we should hold on to the teaching of our old friend, Mohammed Ali, that *to retreat has nothing to do with defeat.*[75]

> *It's hard to stay with ambivalence when one wants to, instinctively, strike back.*
>
> ~ Avital Ronell[76]

Where letting your opponent punch themselves out, wear themselves down, is one of the ways of letting them snatch defeat from the jaws of a seeming victory.

---

[75] Which, once again, doesn't mean there are no costs involved: *rope-a-dope* entails first taking a beating, quite possibly enduring a proper pounding. And lessons, especially the ones that matter, that leave traces, also *mark* one, leave lesions on and in one's body. The *welts* that form our *Weltanschauung*, even our *Welt*. « The scars that write us », as Yanyun Chen would say.

[76] As part of the 'Public Lectures' series hosted by The European Graduate School in which the session on 21 January 2025 was devoted to Avital Ronell's *America: The Troubled Continent of Thought*.

Where, even as there be mourning involved — rememberings, even grievings for, the selves whom they were, that they could have been — there is, simultaneously, an imagining of the selves they might become.

> *I hope it will not be taken amiss if,*
> *upon this universal stage of death,*
> *I venture in turn to open*
> *my paper graveyard.*
>
> ~ Walter Benjamin[77]

Writing themselves into legends.

And, we should try not to forget that to write on paper is always already to write with ashes onto what is dead — a *death on death*; not death as a finality, but which are simultaneously transformative.

東邪西毒.

---

[77] Walter Benjamin, *Origin of a German Trauerspiel*, translated by Howard Eiland. Cambridge: Harvard University Press, 2019, 253.

And as Eduardo Cadava teaches us, « for Benjamin, the act of writing is simultaneously an act of dying and mourning, of living on in the midst of dying ».

Much like art.[78]

Where *Magic|Unfold* — and its accompanying, compendium, side-piece, companion,[79] *Magic Hour* — be nothing other than an attempt to respond to violence with art.

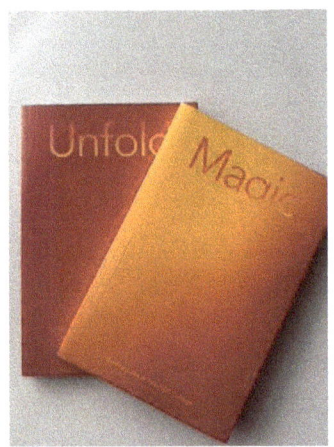

Responses which make no claims to knowing what they are doing, nor reduce

---

[78] For one should try not to forget that all making requires endings — of matter, materials, other possibilities. Much like all living requires dying; and all meals entail murders.

[79] And here one must never forget the importance of *friendship*, of breaking bread (*panis*) together (*com-*), of standing hand-in-hand, in building, making, creating, solidarity.

themselves to goals, objectives, outcomes; that reject the violence inherent in notions like targets, strategies, aims. Where, even as universities have become corporations, *Magic|Unfold* is an attempt to resist the militarisation, the economisation, of art, writing, thinking.

> *Neither painting nor drawing, nor art in general, can achieve anything. It is far removed from colonial appetites and does not even wish to beguile one's contemplation: art does not serve and there are no correspondences, intercessions, or contradictions to be found. This painting, this drawing, is entirely autonomous and engrosses the viewer in a vain search for analogies.*
>
> ~ Hubertus von Amelunxen[80]

For, as Mina Cheon reminds us, « thinkers tinker ».[81]

Play.

While opening themselves to the possibility that what they write, what we write, what is written, will also cause us all to writhe.

---

[80] Hubertus von Amelunxen, *Max Neumann: Some Heads*, translated by Tess Lewis. Calcutta: Seagull Books, 2023, 11.

[81] In response to *America* and to Avital Ronell's opening remarks at the EGS 'Public Lecture' series on 21 January 2025.

Published in English under the title 'News about flowers', the essay's original German title, more literally 'News from flowers', points to the flower's capacity to communicate — to transmit news — and to the need for us to learn how to hear what they wish to tell us. What is so beautiful here is the way in which Walter Benjamin asks us to think about the relations among flowers, plants, persons, images, language, and this because, if these are all related to one another, we perhaps do not yet know what any of them might be. What is at stake, is learning to read ...

- Eduardo Cadava[82]

And, more specifically, learning to read the « image ». And here, we should try not to forget that writing is first and foremost a syntax of images; and visual art always already entails making marks.

And, what are imaginings if not always also images.

Involving *magi*.

And, learning to read paper too: its « good memory » and what it may be holding in

---

[82] Eduardo Cadava, *Paper Graveyards*. Cambridge: The MIT Press, 2021, 451, endnote 2.

store for us; if we take the time to look, to listen, to be in the presence of.

•

Not having the college around is something that everyone — especially those who care about it, have cared for it, will continue to care;[83] perhaps even those who ostensibly have nothing to do with it — will have to readjust to.

> *When one knows that something will soon be removed from one's gaze, that thing becomes an image.*
>
> ~ Walter Benjamin[84]

---

[83] In some way not only is this a question of *curation* — as Yanyun Chen reminds us (« What does one choose to remember, choose to write down, choose to mark ... Whose memories get to remain, and whose left out? And, why? ») — but that *we are all always already curators*, even in, particularly in, our negligence; when we fail to care for, when we are careless, when we decide that something, someone, some other, is lesser, is less deserving to be careful for, about, with.

> *They were careless people, Tom and Daisy — they smashed up things and creatures and then retreated back into their money or their vast carelessness or whatever it was that kept them together, and let other people clean up the mess they had made.*
>
> ~ Nick Carraway

[84] Walter Benjamin, 'The Paris of the Second Empire in Baudelaire', translated by Harry Zohn, in *Selected Writings, vol.4: 1938-1940*, edited by Howard Eiland & Michael W. Jennings. Cambridge: Belknap Press, 2003, 53.

An « act of mourning that remains in love », as Eduardo Cadava might say.[85]

Thankfully, everyone, and every thing, dies twice: once corporeally; another time when one is forgotten. Not necessarily, though, in that sequence.

> *Paper has*
> *a good memory.*
>
> ~ Gordon Koh

Re-adjust.

Which might well also be a call to read-just; and to *just read*.

Reading justly.

> *Let your reading of this anthology*
> *be the forever unfolding of what is yet to come.*
>
> ~ Lawrence Lacambra Ypil

What a ride it's been!

---

[85] Eduardo Cadava, *Paper Graveyards*, 98.

dream sleep[86]

ticktockticktocktick
tockticktockticktock
ticktockticktocktick
tockticktockticktock
ticktockticktocktick
tockticktockticktock
ticktockticktocktick
tockticktockticktock
tickcrosstickcrosstick
crosstickcrosstickcross
tickcrosstickcrosstick
crosstickcrosstickcross
tickcrosstickcrosstick
crosstickcrosstickcross

écrit. cri. écrit
cri. écrit. cri.

.

If power were truly in the hands of the people, surely they should be able to choose whomever they want — a true choice instead of picking from alternatives. And what is more democratic than *writing* the name of whomever one wants in power, regardless of

---

[86] A version of this work was first published with photography by Alice Renez Tay in *Berfrois: Literature, Ideas, Tea*, October 2014. It was also translated as 'Sueña Dormir' by Manuel Bernardo Vargas Ricalde in *Orange Utan Lab*, 2014.

— in spite of — the persons presented on the voting slip. In this manner, regardless of who wins, the symbol chosen by the people *will always haunt the incumbent*. And, not only would the candidate that won through the system be discredited, not only would the democratic system be called into question, the people would have actually spoken.

The people would have actually dreamed.

Perhaps, what we need now is to take the messages that we have been bombarded with — that *nothing is impossible* — seriously. And read it alongside the other message we are not allowed to forget: that the good times are over, that we need to tighten our belts, and most importantly, that *the state owes us nothing*.

And *demand* what we have been owed: *the impossible*.

For, dreams are quite literally worth fighting for. And if they don't let us dream, we won't let them sleep.

my dream is yours ...[87]

ACT I

As I leap off the top rope, aligning my body in a perpendicular fashion to his, suspended in the screams of the crowd, enveloped in the air, floating, drifting in slow motion until our bodies collide, I realise *my future is behind me*.

To pin or not to pin; 'aye there's the rub.

One.

To hold the people in the palm of my hand just a little longer, perhaps one more time, who knows when this will end, when they will stop screaming my name.

Two.

I raise my hand.

---

[87] A version of this work was first published as a chapter in *100 Years of the American Dream: Representations and Conceptions in American Literature, 1919-2019*, edited by Michael Kearney. Newcastle Upon Tyne: Cambridge Scholars Publishing, 2022: 50-77.

One should try never to forget that the crowd is whom you are truly playing to.

> *Wrestling is not a sport,*
> *it is a spectacle ...*
>
> ~ Roland Barthes[88]

Me, my opponent, the referee, setting the stage where you, all of you watching us, in the crowd, in the hall, from afar through the goggle-box, across space and time even, tune yourselves to the stage that is the ring, attune your beings into the squared-circle.

Three.

ting
ting
ting

My hand is raised. Howard Finkel fills my ear: *and the new Intercontinental champion of the world ...*

---

[88] Roland Barthes, 'The World of Wrestling' in *Mythologies*, translated by Annette Lavers. New York: Hill and Wang, 1972, 15.

Dream baby dream
Oh baby you gotta keep those dreams burnin'
Keep them dream burnin forever
Dream baby dream

~ Suicide[89]

ACT I sc. ii

There was a time when one had been free to wrestle anywhere one wanted to, with whomever I wanted to, where being an *independent performer* actually meant something, when the independence lay in where to lace my boots, for whom to put on my tights, and where it was not left up to Vince, to his whims, to cancel my contract whenever he desired, nor to have me belong to him.[90]

---

[89] Martin Reverby & Boruch Bermowitz, 'Dream Baby Dream', single. Right Track Recording, 1979.

[90] **Exclusivity.** This clarifies that all rights granted to WWE are exclusive to the promoter, and that if the wrestler wishes to use either Wrestler IP or New IP in a separate endeavor then he or she must be granted those rights in a sub-license arrangement. All of the available contracts signed from 2000 onward also state that wrestlers are responsible for reimbursing WWE for administrative costs associated with such separate projects, provided that WWE's costs aren't less than 10% of fees received by the wrestler.

Term and Territory. This is straightforward, naming the contract length. In the available documents these range from Sanders' one-year deal to Lesnar's seven-year contract, though WWE's most recent annual report says the company has contracts up to 20 years in length. Some

> *Dream baby*
> *dream.*

Back then, there wasn't a career to be made.

Or maybe there were, but it wasn't something that struck me when I first put on my trunks. When I first stepped into the circle of dreams.

> *Keep the dream*
> *burnin' forever.*

All I wanted was to *superfly*.

---

of the available deals also include automatic one-year renewals. As for territory, that might be the simplest sentence in WWE's legalese: 'The territory of this Agreement shall be the world.'

Chris Smith, 'Breaking down how WWE contracts work' in *Forbes*, March 2015.

ACT II

> *The American dream, that dream of a land in which life should be better and richer and fuller for everyone, with opportunity for each according to ability or achievement. It is a difficult dream for the European upper classes to interpret adequately, and too many of us ourselves have grown weary and mistrustful of it. It is not a dream of motor cars and high wages merely, but a dream of social order in which each man and each woman shall be able to attain to the fullest stature of which they are innately capable, and be recognized by others for what they are, regardless of the fortuitous circumstances of birth or position.*
>
> ~ James Truslow Adams[91]

The trouble with dreams be that they are difficult to see.

The trouble with dreams be that you only see them with your eyes closed. Or glazed over.

I suppose we should have known, pulling up in the steamer heading to what we thought would be a new dawn, expecting to see nothing less than the lady of freedom, and finding, awaiting us, a brothel on Ellis in the shape of an elephant no less.

---

[91] James Truslow Adams, *The Epic of America*. Boston: Little Brown & Company, 1931, 373.

The trouble with dreams be that all you see is yourself.

> *If he's a serial killer, then what's the worst*
> *That could happen to a girl who's already hurt?*
>
> ~ Lana del Rey[92]

And dreams, oh dreams, they might well deceive you, delude you, keep your head in the clouds so that an apparition might find you, so that a ghost could speak to you. Even as all you hear might well be *voices in your head.*[93]

Especially if she might be whispering *remember me.*

Just because we like to think dreams are from the future, are-to-come, who's to say they haven't already happened, that we

---

[92] Elizabeth Grant, Jack Antonoff, & Richard Nowels, 'Happiness is A Butterfly' in Lana del Rey, *Norman Fucking Rockwell*. London & Santa Monica, Interscope Records & Polydor Records, 2018.

[93] **Dream**, (*traum*, from the German).

Perhaps from the Proto-Germanic **draugmas* 'deception, illusion, phantasm' (source also of Old Saxon *bidriogan*, Old High German *triogan*, German *trügen* 'to deceive, delude,' Old Norse *draugr* 'ghost, apparition'). Possible cognates outside Germanic are Sanskrit *druh-* 'seek to harm, injure,' Avestan *druz-* 'lie, deceive'.

might have missed it, or that they are happening right now, just that they weren't quite the dream we wanted.

Just because you dream it, think you're the one doing the dreaming, doesn't mean she can't tell you to *dream on.*

For who's to say that *remember me* is only a plea: it could well also be a question, might well be said mockingly. Trouble being, only you can tell; it's all in how you say it to yourself — not that you have any control over how it comes to you.

So not so much that you were lied to — more like you lied, are constantly lying, to yourself.

Even in the moment in which it were the elephant you were seeing.

All whilst lying down.
How else to read, *sauf sur un lit.*

ACT II sc. ii

*I lie, I cheat,
I steal.*

~ Eddie Guerrero[94]

Where any reading of the world of wrestling should not, really cannot, ignore the shift, the move — *translation* — from *sport* into *sport-entertainment*.

Not just to avoid the regulations from athletic commissions.[95]

And their accompanying taxes — and in many ways, what is more American than that: this was exemplified in the refusal of both major parties, and many of their members, to support Bernie Sanders in both his 2016 and 2020 presidential-campaigns. For any gesture, let alone an attempt to

---

[94] Jim Johnston, 'Viva la raza', theme song for Eddie Guerrero. WWE, 2016.

[95] David Bixenspan, 'Thirty Years Ago, WWE Admitted It Wasn't A Sport To Try And Dodge Regulations', in *Deadspin: Sports News without Fear, Favour, or Compromise*, February 2019.

Richard Hoy-Browne, 'Historic Moments in Wrestling part 6: Vince McMahon admits wrestling is predetermined', in *The Independent*, May 2014.

enact higher taxation — let alone open the possibility of *a commons* — is anathema to the general American consciousness. The memes after Joe Biden's inauguration in January 2021, which had Sanders in every conceivable place, almost seemed to confirm the fact that *we'll put Bernie everywhere except in the White House.*

But more importantly that it holds a mirror up to anyone who watches sport: we watch not so much for the sportive elements but to be entertained.

For, no one really watches NASCAR to see who wins the race, even less to bear witness to the skill of the drivers manoeuvering around the track, but for the crashes — for the point when the cars come together, ideally in a hail of sparks and flames; for the moment when there is no actual race taking place.

That we are spectators because we want a *spectacle.*

But, no one must actually get hurt.

For death, or a serious injury, ruptures the show, shatters the screen, only reminds us —

makes it too real to us — that the ones who dance for us are *human, all too human*.

> *We don't need another hero*
> *We don't need to know the way home*
> *All we want is life beyond the Thunderdome*
>
> ~ Tina Turner[96]

For who could adore another human being — with her complexities, his flaws, their similarities to ourselves.

But *a puppet or a God* ...

---

[96] Terry Britten & Graham Lyle, 'We don't need another hero (Thunderdome)' in *Mad Max Beyond Thunderdome: Original Motion Picture Soundtrack*. Capitol, 1985.

ACT II sc. iii

Entertain
(verb)

to hold together (*entretenir*)
to hold (*tenir*), among (*entre-*)

And here, one should try not to forget that the crowd, the masses of people, the public — the elusive *hearts and minds* — were won over not in the Senate, but in the heat of the Colosseum.

> *I said, 'Don't be a jerk, don't call me a taxi'*
> *Sitting in your sweatshirt, crying in the backseat*
> *Ooh, I just wanna dance with you*
>
> ~ Lana del Rey[97]

---

[97] Lana del Rey, 'Happiness is A Butterfly'.

ACT II sc. iv

And what better way to hold everyone together — to build, form, coalesce, construct, « a dream of a social order » — than with a secret, particularly a dirty little secret.

For, one should bear in mind — even if it remains a burden on one, especially if it bears down on one — that *something is only a secret if it is shared*: if you are the only one who knows it, it is merely something known; and it is only at the point where two or more know it — and, more importantly, when those in the know agree that others must not know, have to be excluded from knowing this — that it moves into the realm of a secret. Where, the object of the secret is less important than its significance as secret. For knowing my mother's maiden name is irrelevant unless you also know that it is the password to my bank account.

And, more importantly, a public disavowal of — a silence, even silencing, in the *polis* about — this secret.

Which is why Thanksgiving only entails turkeys, families, gatherings, but not its accompanying genocide.

Much like Columbus Day.

And pornography — privately consumed, even shared, whilst publicly decried or never spoken of.

For, it exposes too clearly how the relationship between people — and, by extension, the state, which is nothing other than the social ordering of people — functions. After all, all porn films are virtually the same; the only difference being the actors involved. Which suggests the performers are inter-changeable; it really makes no difference who is playing that role. In fact, it foregrounds the very nature of roles itself. Where, in each porn flick one can hear an echo of « all the world's a stage / and all the men and women merely players »[98] — and this is precisely the reason it will always be marginalised in any society: it reminds us too honestly of the fact that everyone is exchangeable, ourselves included. And there is nothing more

---

[98] William Shakespeare, *As You Like It*, Act II Scene VII, Line 139

anathema to the standard reading of « we hold these truths to be self-evident, that all men are created equal »[99] — that each person is unique — than to open the register that the 'equalness' refers to 'interchangeable', to being *just another brick in the wall*.[100]

And, regardless of the size and age of any nation state, it cannot afford to have its fundamental illusory premises exposed.

This was very clearly illustrated in New York City on Monday morning of 27 April 2009. On said day, there was pandemonium when planes flying over Lower Manhattan, Staten Island, and Jersey City, caused scores of people to rush from their office buildings. As *The New York Times* reports, « the low-flying Boeing 747 speeded in the shadows of skyscrapers, trailed by two fighter jets ... awakened barely dormant fears of a terrorist attack, causing a momentary panic that sent workers pouring out of buildings on both

---

[99] *Declaration of Independence*, 1776:
https://www.archives.gov/founding-docs/declaration-transcript

[100] Roger Waters, 'Another Brick in the Wall' in Pink Floyd, *The Wall*, Los Angeles: Harvest Records, 1979.

sides of the Hudson River ».¹⁰¹

The irony of it being: this was Air Force One flying over the New York City skyline to allow officials to take photographs near the Statue of Liberty for publicity purposes. Then-President Obama was said to be furious: of course he would have been — never has the impotence of the United States at countering the terrorist threat been so openly displayed. The fact that it was Air Force One with two military jets trailing it cemented this even further: clearly nothing in the skies over New York can ever be trusted again. One might even go as far as to posit that the terror of Air Force One over New York was not just brought on by the ghost of September 11 2001, but even more so by the spectres of Timothy McVeigh, Terry Nichols, and the Oklahoma City bombings of 1995. Where, at the moment the terror spread over New York, when people fled from buildings and « ran like hell », what happened was the exposure of not only the fact that the United States would never be safe again, can never be safe from a well-planned attack, but even more

---

[101] A. G. Sulzberger and Matthew L. Wald, 'Jet Flyover Frightens New Yorkers', in *The New York Times*, April 2009.

so that it was always most at risk from itself. And this is quite possibly why the 2nd Amendment can never be discussed, let alone debated, without bringing forth intense emotions: not because it is a right to militia and defense from the state (for, who genuinely believes they can challenge, fight, let alone overcome, the might of the American military-industrial complex) but that weapons, mass-shootings, pillaging, were precisely the foundations on which the United States of America is built.

The mistake made by the officials in New York was in attempting to demonstrate they owned the skies again, that all was safe.

And, all they managed to do was shatter that very illusion.

For, in order to maintain illusions, one has to maintain a proper distance — sometimes this takes the form of a gap of silence. Where, whomever orchestrated the flyover forgot was the fact that silence, this gap, is precisely what gives the space for the ones who see, the spectators, to imbue the skies with whatever they want.

And, it is not that we can't tell *blue skies from pain(t)*,¹⁰² but that we won't if we don't want to.

Which is why the 2ⁿᵈ Amendment might stand a chance to be amended again not only when the relationship between a 'free-state' and the 'right to bear arms', when the idea binding the two notions, is un-linked, but — perhaps more importantly — when the myth of 'moving West', conquering land, taming the flora and fauna (and, one should remember that the indigenous peoples were seen as savages, animals), is altered.

Where the tale of civilising the natives is now, one might even say finally, seen as a murder — thus, un-American.

For, no one has ever been convinced solely by facts. And, even if you manage to conquer (*vincere*) them, become a victor over them, even vanquish them, you would never have won them over unless they choose to come with (*com-*), be together with, stand alongside, you.

---

¹⁰² David Gilmour & Roger Waters, 'Wish You Were Here' in *Wish You Were Here*. Harvest, 1975.

So much the better if they feel like they are breathing (*spirare*) with (*con-*) you, conspiring with you, in spirit with you.

> *I wanna do bad things*
> *with you.*
>
> ~ Jace Everett[103]

> *Vice involves a complicity more profound and immediate than any verbal communication. It suffuses the body instantaneously like an inner melody, completely transmogrifying mind, flesh, and blood.*
>
> ~ Max Blecher[104]

Where is why what is supposedly a *moral fault*, a *wickedness*, is often also what brings bodies together, holds them together, in a vice-like grip; where it is these so-called defects, blemishes, imperfections, *vitium*, that draws everyone in — is precisely the source of entertainment (*vezzo*).

---

[103] Jace Everett, 'Bad Things' in *Jace Everett*. Epic Nashville, 2005.

[104] Max Blecher, *Adventures in Immediate Irreality*, translated by Michael Henry Helm, New York: New Direction Books, 2105: 18

After all, there's nothing better than a freak show to make the rest of us — those who gawk, who watch, who peep, spy; bathing ourselves in secret, thus shared, shame — feel normal; lets us all hold on to the illusion that we are sane.

Regardless of what we watch, whom we see, who we vote for.

ACT III

*Long ago, and, oh, so far away
I fell in love with you before the second show*

~ The Carpenters[105]

Save him ... was the only thought occupying his mind as he rode in. 'He's the last of the noblemen, even if he doesn't quite seem to know it himself these days.'
'If he doesn't know it, can he be all that noble?' replied the ass. 'Surely nobility would imply that you knew what you are doing!'
'Certainly! Why else would he be making those claims to save the nation? Repair the economy in spite of all mathematical facts? He's all the more noble for marching straight into the unknown.'
'Adderall baby.'
'No wonder you're just longing for tomatoes', muttered the rider.
'If you're unhappy, go ride a bloody elephant.'

He had to bite his tongue.

---

[105] Bonnie Bramlett, Leon Russell, & Delaney Bramlett, 'Groupie (Superstar)', B-side single. Atlantic Records, 1969.

The storm was, around him, flying. Wooden backyard fences had broken-off and an outdoor glass table was dancing with the devil. And as far as he could tell, the storm hadn't even properly hit. To console himself, he entertained thoughts of the man running through the streets, raining curses — cursing rains — as the wind was messing with his hair. At least it was better than muttering clichés about not being able to go on whilst actually moving ...

'Why are you doing this?'
'Memories ...'
'Of him? He who made you ride behind him, walk behind him, be behind him?'
'Not so much him but his ideas. Wanting to rid the world of naysayers, evildoers, wanting to save all womenfolk from corruption, from the ways of the world. Challenging anyone, and everyone, in his path who didn't match his ideals.'

However, riding was no longer good enough for the Don. He had now dedicated himself exclusively to the Bugatti Royale. Had rejected the Rolls Royce completely: it was inconceivable, in his mind, that in front of every man was a woman.

An elephant on the other hand:
that couldn't be put into binders.

Sometimes, he wondered if Lincoln wasn't actually assassinated. Being a visionary he might have caught a glimpse of what his party would be turned into — and shot, he just let himself be.

ACT III sc. ii

don't you worry
i've got your back
i sometimes need
something to stab

~ Zhang Jieqiang[106]

---

[106] Unpublished poem.

ACT III sc. iii

*Your guitar, it sounds so sweet and clear
But you're not really here, it's just the radio.*

~ The Carpenters

The Don had caught wind his old squire was on the way. Ordinarily, he wouldn't have been in the least bothered. He practically had him on a leash, had him tail-him without questioning — even had him walk behind his horse after his donkey had been nicked.

His loyalty was infinite.

Earlier that month he had even sent a note saying he was going to come, try one last time to convince him to come back on the road. That he had strayed from his noble path: that people mattered. *Typical humanist bullshit*, muttered the Don. He was about to crush the note and consign it to the bins when his eye the flipside caught.

That poem disturbed him for days.

He cursed his upbringing — if he were being rational, would have seen it as just the back of a note, should have fired that squire sooner for not even writing on blank paper.

But now, poetic premonition was haunting him.

ACI III sc. iv

Treacherous Fernando! You'll now, this instant, pay for the wrong you've did to me! With my hands I'll tear out that wicked heart of yours that is filled with every crime, especially with fraud and trickery!

~ Miguel de Cervantes[107]

---

[107] Miguel de Cervantes Saavedra, *Don Quixote*, translated by Walter Starkie, with an introduction by Eward H. Friedman. New York: Signet Classic, 2001: 228.

ACT III sc. v

Don't you remember, you told me you loved me, baby?
You said you'd be coming back this way again, baby
Baby, baby, baby, baby, oh baby
I love you, I really do

- The Carpenters

What always disturbed Sancho was his insistence that one day he would be King. Whilst they were riding together, he had hoped that this perhaps were just his twin within talking — his nemesis, as it were.

'You are hoping against hope you know', he heard his ass mutter.
'Then why are you coming along then?'
'You're asking the one who is harnessed?!', came the reply, almost instantly, filled with incredulity.
'Ah yes, sorry', sighed Sancho, 'I did pick up some bad habits after all.'

'I don't really think it's him though.'
'Why'ja say that?', came the reply from beneath.
'I think it's really his image.'

'But don't they all just end up falling in love with their own reflections — even Narcissus did.'
'Only when he didn't know it was his self.'
'Maybe then what you need to do is to show him himself.'
'Like Brutus?'
'Perhaps ...'

'Anything you know that might catch his attention?'
'He ...', said the rider reticently, 'has a *strange hobby — collecting clothes, moonshine, washing line.*'
'What — like Arnold?'
'*Takes two to know, two to know ...*'[108]

'Hang on', said the ass, 'he wants to rule the world, you want to save the world. Pray tell, what is the difference?'
'What we ride on ...'

Amo aquella vez como si fuera la última ...[109]

---

[108] Syd Barrett. 'Arnold Layne', Columbia (EMI), 1967. Vinyl.

[109] I love that time as if it were the last ...

ACT IV

Artificiality seemed to enable the actors presenting them to comprehend the mystification of the world involved ... in a world that is all theatre, all backdrop, life must be presented in a false ornamental fashion.

~ Max Blecher[110]

And it is not as if the audience even needs any conscious *suspension of disbelief* — after all, *all the world's a stage*. And they know that regardless of the fixed nature of the match, it is them, and only them, which decides its actual outcome; significance.

Which might have been why our matches were always more real than unscripted MMA fights: those were left up to chance; and which self-respecting American didn't believe they were above that.

Wrestling is a sum of spectacles, of which no single one is a function ...

~ Roland Barthes[111]

---

[110] Max Blecher, *Adventures in Immediate Irreality*, 36.

[111] Roland Barthes, 'The World of Wrestling', 16.

Which is precisely why it is *le monde où l'on catche* : for, wrestling has nothing to do with a fight (*une lutte*) — anyone can win or lose that.

> ... *each moment imposes the total knowledge of a passion which rises erect and alone, without ever extending to the crowning moment of a result.*[112]

Wrestling is nothing other than destiny.

And not some banal one left to providence, due to some « fortuitous circumstance of birth or position », but a *personal destiny*, one that was *written for you and you alone*, in which you reach « the fullest stature » of yourself.

> *He's just a common working hard with his hands,*
> *He's just a common man working hard for the man.*
> *Hey He's Amerrrrrrrrrrriiccann Dreammm.*
>
> ~ Dusty Rhodes[113]

And when I walk down the aisle, it is you who are walking down not with me, but *in*

---

[112] *ibid*, 16.

[113] Jimmy Hart & J.J. Maguire, 'Common Man Boogie', entrance song for Dusty Rhodes.

me — where *you are me*. Where, regardless of the song that is playing, in our ears we hear Doris Day whispering *my dream is yours*.

Hence, the importance of *kayfabe*: which is the very lesson Donald Trump learnt whilst he was with us.

Never break character, no matter what.

For, as Stalin taught us, the moment appearances are ruptured, reality itself collapses. And, it is not just that one has to agree with Stalin all the time, one also has to maintain the illusion that free discourse is possible; otherwise the fantasy that Stalin has been freely chosen to lead the people — that he is the first servant, as it were — is destroyed.

And the whole game comes crumbling down.[114]

---

[114]

> *All transgressions are possible, but not the infraction of the rule.*
>
> ~ Jean Baudrillard

And what is this rule that has been *infracted* — that has been fractured?

Nothing other than *the fantasy that it is the leader that leads*. For, if it is the people who are propping up not just the leader (everyone already knows that) but the very *notion* of the leader itself, then reality — where

Which is what truly scares us: not just that the leader we're following might have been *us* (with all our failings), but that *the leader is us*; that we have imbued the leader, the one we follow, with our fantasies of what it is to be a leader.

Which is why there is nothing more appropriate than strains of Elgar accompanying Randy Savage as he struts down the arena. And, in that moment, he is not only no longer Randall Mario Poffo, but that we have transformed him, perhaps even trans-substantiated him — for, it is not as if there is any material, phenomenal, difference between Poffo and Savage — into *The Macho Man* in all of his *pomp and circumstance*. And, perhaps more importantly, that it is *with him* — us and him together — that takes flight off the top-rope for that elbow drop to bring us to the *land of hope and glory*.

---

there is a leader and followers; and, even more importantly, that there is a difference between the one who leads and those who follow — crumbles.

*Knock knock knockin
On heaven's door*

~ Bob Dylan[115]

ACT IV sc. ii

I believe that theatre, like life, is made up of the unbroken conflict between impressions and judgments — illusion and disillusion cohabit painfully and are inseparable ... Everything about this play is designed to crack the spectator on the jaw, then douse him with ice-cold water, then force him to assess intelligently what has happened to him, then give him a kick in the balls, then bring him back to his senses again ...

~ Peter Brook[116]

Like a chair shot ...

---

[115] Bob Dylan, 'Knocking on Heaven's Door' in *Pat Garrett & Billy the Kid*, New York: Columbia Records, 1973.

[116] Peter Brook, 'Introduction' in Peter Weiss, *Marat/Sade: the persecution and assassination of Marat as performed by the inmates of the asylum of Charenton under the direction of the Marquis de Sade*, adapted into the English by Geoffrey Skelton & Adrian Mitchell. London: Marion Boyars, 1965, ii.

ACT IV sc. iii

Which might well by why there was nothing more appropriate than Donald Trump becoming the 45th President of the United States:[117] not only because he was clearly tax-avoiding, rule-bending, law-ignoring (which is the manifestation of not just the outlaw and the sheriffs, but captures the very essence of the Western itself), but that he allows us to live our fantasies of 'draining the swamp', 'bringing down the establishment', 'giving the finger to the man', through him. And here, we should recall the fact that the pivotal moment in American detective movies is the scene where the protagonist throws his badge into the urinal, when he becomes an outlaw — in the literal sense of *stepping outside the boundaries of the law* — in order to solve the crime.

As if *justice* can only come from *beyond the pale*.

---

[117] The fact that Trump is also the 47th President should not be lost on us here: for it demonstrates not just a quirk of convention (that if one does not hold office for consecutive terms one is considered a 'new' president) but — more importantly — that it is not a person as such who holds office, but a figure. That (in this case Donald J. Trump, but also Grover Cleveland) there only needs be a body there, for the president is a *figure*, nothing more and infinitely nothing less.

So, not just a justice outside of the confines of the law, or community (which is why any mention of socialism, or *the commons*, brings on a case of the heebie-jeebies) but that *justice is self-defined.*

As, apparently are elections.

Usually regarded as an expression of the will of the people, of the *polis* — but now, it is not just that 'I was defrauded' (which would still maintain the logic of people getting to choose, would still rely on the notion of the *kratos* of the *demos*) but a *I won because I say I won*.[118]

Where, Trump is the perfect manifestation of being able to attain *fullest stature of which* [*you*] *are innately capable* — bearing in mind that this 'innateness' has nothing to do with ability and capability, but is a question of *what is within*; thus, solipsistic.

I can be whatever I want me to be; another, more contemporary, manifestation of this being the oft-repeated mantra, *living my best life*.

---

[118] Alongside: 'it is fair when I win, otherwise not'; so no longer a game which determines the outcome, but nor just that I can define the game, but — as Triple H would say — « I am the game ».

And, it is no longer that *the truth is out there* — move over Mulder and Scully —, nor just *the truth is in me*, but *I am the way, the truth, and the light.*

Whenever I want [to]
All I have to do
is dream, dream dream dream.

~ The Everly Brothers, jf remix[119]

---

[119] Boudleaux Bryant, 'All I Have To Do is Dream' in The Everly Brothers, *Claudette*, B-side single, New York: Cadence Records, 1958.

ACT V

Well, I'll be damned
Here comes your ghost again
But that's not unusual
It's just that the moon is full
And you happened to call.

- Joan Baez[120]

One never quite walks away from the circle of dreams.

I suspect that's why we all put-over in, lose our, final match: the performer steps away but the show, *the show, must go on.*[121]

---

[120] Joan Baez, 'Diamonds and Rust' in *Diamonds and Rust*, Santa Monica: A&M Records, 1975.

[121] This is why it is possible for the same gimmick to continue with a different wrestler: Buddy Rogers, Ric Flair, and Buddy Landel, all performed as 'The Nature Boy' (the latter two at the same time, within the same organisation, no less); at least 8 different wrestlers, most famously Satoru Sayama, have donned the 'Tiger Mask' persona. And it is not always the so-called original who is best-known: Óscar Gutiérrez Rubio who wrestles under the name of 'Rey Mysterio' — taking-over the eagle themed mask and tights from his uncle, Miguel Ángel López Díaz — has become so synonymous with his wrestling moniker that the latter has since renamed himself 'Rey Mysterio Sr'.

The same wrestler can also play multiple characters, sometimes even within the same show: arguably the best-known instance of this occurred during the 1998 Royal Rumble where Mick Foley performed as 3 different characters: Cactus Jack, Mankind, and Dude Love.

People think we drink to cope with the pain, to deal with the bumps and bruises, fractures and falls, with the loneliness of being on the road, with the insecurities of a contract that may be abruptly cancelled, with a lifetime of work that might be ruptured by an accidental fall, a fist erroneously placed, a slip off the cage, a ladder which fails to hold up, a *finishing hold* which actually ends it all.

> *We drink — be it alcohol, caffeine, or water — to slip into our own skin. When we drink, we seek to become more of ourselves, to modify and alter our chemistry; it is an act of solvency, to absolve, to solve, to find a solution. We drink to dilute and concentrate in response to the world around us.*
>
> *~ Sara Chong*[122]

But perhaps, each time I take a sip of my gin, the voice of Sara Chong echoes, her wise words resound, in my ear.

I drink to lose my body: not because I don't want to feel — nothing that banal — but to open myself to the world, to let it into me, to permeate every pore of myself with each cheer, any jeer, laughter, tears, shriek, scream, sound, gesture, moment ...

---

[122] Sara Chong, wall-text as part of the group-show *Still, Singapore Life*, Singapore: Art Seasons Gallery, 2018.

I love crowds: they let me be me, alone —
and with them. Part of and apart from them.

Where my *gimmick* is not merely a character
— *babyface*, fan-favourite, someone to hate,
heel — but also a portal for you to travel,
with me. Which is also why multiple people
can have, share, the same role; all whilst
making it their own.

Same same but different.

Where perhaps the gap between each one
playing the role is but an *interregnum*.

Merely awaiting inauguration —
not from any authority, for we are no longer
in the realm of the gods, or the state, nor any
governing institution.

But the people.

ACT V sc. ii

Squared-circle: where it is named so not just because of its shape, of the fact that the ropes surrounding it make it so, nor merely to differentiate it from amateur wrestling which happens in a circle-shaped mat, but that the four-walls *transforms* our ring into a stage.

And here, one should try not to forget that even as we go by the name 'professional wrestlers' the fact that we are being paid has never changed the fact that we always will be *amateurs*, that there is love (*amore*) in and for what we do — that it is in 'wrestling' that the transformation occurs, in its movement, in its translation, from *sport* to *theatre*.

Thus, life.

> *What's love got to do, got to do with it?*
> *What's love but a second hand emotion?*
> *What's love got to do, got to do with it?*
> *Who needs a heart, when a heart can be broken.*
>
> ~ Tina Turner[123]

---

[123] Terry Britten & Graham Lyle, 'What's Love Got To Do With It', in Tina Turner, *Private Dancer*. Los Angeles: Capitol Records, 1984.

How does one walk away from the squared-circle?

Which is the same question as *how does one walk-off the stage*, not overstay one's welcome, not have one match too many, put myself on show one-time too much.

> *And how can you mend a broken heart?*
> *How can you stop the rain from falling down?*
> *How can you stop the sun from shining?*
> *What makes the world go round?*
> *How can you mend this broken man?*
> *How can a loser ever win?*
> *Please help me mend my broken heart and let me live again.*
>
> ~ The Bee Gees[124]

How do I leave such that the audience wants more, wants more of me, wants me more, such that they still *continue to dream of me when I am no longer there.*

---

[124] Barry Gibb & Robin Gibb, 'How Can You Mend A Broken Heart', A-side single, London: Polydor Records, 1971.

> *Disappearing should be an art form, a seductive way of leaving the world. I believe that part of disappearing is to disappear before you die, to disappear before you have run dry, while you still have something to say ...*
>
> ~ Jean Baudrillard[125]

After all, to become *legendary* one has to enter the realm of stories (*legenda*), become something to be read (*legere*), be transformed into a tale to be told to others, to be told by others ...

... to be *transubstantiated* into a tale others are willing to tell.

And in disappearing, one does nothing other than to leave a space for others to fill with their version — their *fantasy* — of you.

*I can be whatever
you want me to be.*

Where you become legion.

Dream-story.

---

[125] Truls Lie, 'The art of disappearing: an interview with Jean Baudrillard', in *Eurozine*, April 2007.

My dream stretches like a fine skin over my body and over the state of my sleep at the moment. One might even say I am awake. I am awake through sleep and dreaming my wakefulness at the same moment I am dreaming my sleep.

~ Max Blecher[126]

My dream is yours.

ACT V sc. iii

The idea of the play is the play itself, and this cannot be resolved in a simple slogan.

~ Peter Brook

A dream is a dream is a dream.

But in your dreams whatever they be,
Dream a little dream of me.

~ Doris Day[127]

---

[126] Max Blecher, *Adventures in Immediate Irreality*, 115.

[127] Fabian Andre, Wilbur Schwandt, & Gus Kahn, 'Dream A Little Dream Of Me', A-side single, New York: Brunswick Records, 1931.

ACT V sc. iv

> *To the withering of the individual man*
> *and a slow merging into uniformity,*
> *to the death of choice,*
> *to self-denial,*
> *to deadly weakness*
> *in a state*
> *which has no contact with individuals*
> *but which is impregnable.*
> *So I turn away.*
>
> ~ Le Marquis de Sade in *Marat/Sade*[128]

For, it is not as if *dreaming a dream* means it will happen to you.

Or, that you get what you desire.

But, the worst being, when you realise *your dream isn't the dream you should be dreaming*; that yours is the *wrong dream*.

The problem with *the American Dream* being the article: for, whoever said that there could only be one.

Or, worse still, the fact that 'each man and each woman' can have the dream that is 'innate' to them suggests that, regardless of

---

[128] Peter Weiss, *Marat/Sade*, 57.

everyone's attempts, *only one* can have it at any given moment.

Or, perhaps more tragically, that your dream, the dream that comes to you, calls out to you, that is 'innate' to you, that you have worked so hard to achieve, given up everything for, sacrificed the rest of your life to, let go of all-other-possibilities for, is *un-American*.

Who gets to say,
'aye there's the rub!

> *Your poetry's bad*
> *and you blame the news*
>
> ~ Lana del Rey[129]

Where, *the American dreamer*, the dreaming American, is one who never makes the mistake of trying to make their dreams fit reality, but instead *writes the world into their dream*.

---

[129] Elizabeth Grant & Jack Antonoff, 'Norman Fucking Rockwell in Lana del Rey, *Norman Fucking Rockwell*, 2018.

American reality has been so extreme of late that satire is almost impossible. Anything you could possibly imagine actually happens. It would stump Jonathan Swift.

~ Fran Leibowitz[130]

*Everyone knows
I won the election.*

Bigly.

---

[130] Sean O'Hagan, 'Fran Lebowitz: I am really not a contrarian' in *The Guardian*, February 2021.

ACT V sc. v

But what do I know —
it disappears like everything does,
especially dreams.

> *It vanished when the Bastille fell,*
> *it vanished as everything written.*
> *Everything thought and planned*
> *will disappear.*
>
> ~ Le Marquis de Sade in *Marat/ Sade*[131]

This might well be why the enduring image of the United States is not its cities, but Route 66, its highways, more specifically with one in a car, on a bike, embarking on an endless journey, cruising along a *lost highway*.

Not so much because one is looking for a future that is to-come, a dream of a future, a futurial-dream, not just because the dream is to be on the road, but that *the dream is the road itself*.

Not heading anywhere, just moving —
a horse with no name.

---

[131] Peter Weiss, *Marat/Sade*, 88.

Where the American dream is not a place, a thing, but a movement, a transit, constantly transferring, a transference, in-between places, spaces, things, peoples, in translation ...

... *trans-* ...

> *America ducks the question of origins;*
> *it cultivates no origin or mythical authenticity;*
> *it has no past and no founding truth.*
> *Having known no primitive accumulation of time,*
> *it lives in a perpetual present.*
>
> ~ Jean Baudrillard[132]

I can be whatever
you want me to be.

---

[132] Jean Baudrillard, 'Utopia Achieved' in *America*, translated by Chris Turner, with an introduction by Geoff Dyer, London: Verso, 2010, 74.

Even in this day and age, we revere truth. But at the same time, we devote ourselves to the task of erasing the distinction between truth and fiction.

~ IZUMI SUZUKI

Power itself must be abolished — and not solely because of a refusal to be dominated, which is at the heart of all traditional struggles — but also, just as violently, in the refusal to dominate. Intelligence cannot, can never be in power because intelligence consists of this double refusal.

~ JEAN BAUDRILLARD

ESTRAGON

The desire to be taken seriously is precisely what compels people to follow the tried and true paths of knowledge production ... The queer art of failure turns on the impossible, the improbable, the unlikely, and the unremarkable. It quietly loses, and in losing it imagines other goals for life, for love, for art, and for being.

~ J. JACK HALBERSTAM

*Did you exchange
a walk on part in the war
for a lead role in a cage?*

~ PINK FLOYD

Freedom: DADA DADA DADA, the howl of clashing colours, the intertwining of all contradictions, grotesqueries, trivialities: LIFE.

~ TRISTAN TZARA

mandalay

                    Pagoda, lookin'   at the sea,
      Burma
      wind   in   palm-trees,   temple-bells

Where the flyin'-fishes play,
An' the dawn comes up like thunder outer China
'crost the Bay!

                                      Theebaw

> Look down the barrel of a gun and
> feel the moon replace the sun
>
> Everything we've ever stolen
> Has been lost, returned or broken
> No more dragons left to slay
>
>   - Robbie Williams,
>   *The Road to Mandalay*

    the mist   on the rice-fields an' the
sun   droppin' slow,

Elephints a-pilin' teak
In the   creek,

On the road to Mandalay ...

them spicy garlic smells,
An' the sunshine an'   palm-trees an' the   temple-bells;
On the road to Mandalay...

          neater, sweeter   cleaner, greener land
               Mandalay...

               no Ten Commandments an
   t;
For the temple-bells are callin', an' it's there that I would be
By the old Moulmein Pagoda, looking   at the sea;

                                              Mandalay!
O the road to Mandalay,
Where the flyin'-fishes play,
An' the dawn comes up like thunder outer China 'crost the Bay !

~ R   K

half a world apart brings us closer ...
twirling-alongside *Dancing Without Touching*
by Sarah Choo Jing[133]

ACT I

> *Unfettered spaces scare me.*
> *I'm not used to scenes*
> *that aren't in the frame ...*
> *It's probably from all the TV.*
>
> ~ Izumi Suzuki[134]

to dance,
perchance to dream ...

Keeping in mind that dreams come to one, envelop one, quite possibly take over one, take one over, overtake one — and not only does one never quite have control over a dream, it might well write itself into one in ways that will always remain beyond one's knowledge.

A dream writing; an unreadable writing; perhaps an invisible writing; or maybe a

---

[133] A version of this work was first published in *Philosophy World Democracy* in April 2023.

[134] Izumi Suzuki, 'Terminal Boredom' in *Terminal Boredom: Stories*, translated by Daniel Joseph, London: Verso, 2021, 191.

writing that is awaiting reading. And where the effects of said writing are precisely its traces unveiling itself — waiting to be read.

Where perhaps *to dance is to risk being in the realm of the unknown* — in the *oikos* of the *idiotes*.

Stumbling around in the dark.

And in that darkness, what is perhaps being dreamt of is space; a « space » that, as Jean-Luc Nancy continues to teach us, « is first needed for touch ».[135]

To touch, to think, to thank: *ein Denken, das immer auch ein Danken ist*.[136] With thanks to Martin Heidegger for the reminder that to think (*denken*) is to thank (*sich bedanken*), perhaps especially when said « thinking touches on a sphere ».[137]

---

[135] This line first came to me during Jean-Luc Nancy's seminar, *Art, Community, & Politics*, at The European Graduate School in June 2006.

[136] The echo of *danke* in *danken* was first brought to my ears in a conversation with Avital Ronell on the slopes of Saas Fee in August 2014.

[137] Martin Heidegger, 'The Origin of the Work of Art' in *Poetry, Language, Thought*, translated by Albert Hofstadter, New York: Harper Perennial, 2001, 59.

Or a disco ball.

After all, *being thankful as we think* should at least could, hopefully would, bring on a smile.

Ah, *to think with a smile*: that might even bring us a touch of joy, even as, as John Lennon might well continue to say « happiness is a warm gun »[138]: hopefully whilst dancing on a bed with Yoko Ono.

Mmm Fluxus.

Tout est art

~ Ben Vautier[139]

---

[138] John Lennon & Paul McCartney, 'Happiness is a Warm Gun' in *The Beatles*, London: Apple, 1968.

[139] Ben Vautier, *Tout est art*, Oil and mixed technique on Canvas, 1970.

ACT I sc. ii

Dance is the only art of which we ourselves are the stuff of which it is made. Dancing is like dreaming with your feet!

~ Constanze Mozart[140]

Dancing is silent poetry.

~ Simonides[141]

What is dance?

What can you reply, in general, to human questions?

~ Michel Houellebecq[142]

---

[140] This is something she allegedly said, or at least has been attributed to her over time; so, apocryphal ... like the best tales always are.

[141] This thought is attributed to Simonides by Plutarch in his essay 'De gloria Atheniensium' ('On the glory of the Athenians'), beyond which it is impossible to verify, even more delicious for being so.

[142] Michel Houellebecq, *The Map and The Territory*, translated by Gavin Bowd, London: William Heinemann, 2011, 148.

ACT I sc. iii

Sarah Choo Jing
Dancing Without Touching
2023
5-Channel Video Installation
Duration: 7 minutes

ACT I sc. iv

There is a whole art in unfurling a body of thought in such a way that one ends up passing it by without seeing it. This is the opposite of discourse, which lays out its findings and arguments and sentences itself to house arrest within the precincts of its own conclusions ...

~ Jean Baudrillard[143]

A drawing is simply a line going for a walk.

~ Paul Klee[144]

To walk, to wander,
perchance to wonder ... ah, to drift,
to dream.

---

[143] I first had the pleasure of encountering this thought as a line on a wall during the *fête* celebrating the life and works of Jean Baudrillard — in commemoration of a decade of his passing — which was organised by Marine Dupuis Baudrillard in Paris, June 2017.

[144] It is of significance, at least to me, that this thought was first brought to me by an artist, my dear friend Yanyun Chen, in response to my question, « what, to you, is drawing? » : both for the wonderful notion from Paul Klee but also for the fact that her notion of drawing had come to her, walked over to her as it were, from another, from her encounter with this thought, a thought that not only drew her towards it but has clearly also drawn itself into her, as it has now on me.

To further explore Klee's vision of drawing, please see Paul Klee, *Pedagogical Sketchbook*, translated and with an introduction by Sibyl Moholy-Nagy, New York: Praeger Publishers, 1960, in which the idea of « line going for a walk » is demonstrated, toyed-around-with, played-out.

Dériver : but *from* — *to* — *what? Et, où et quand arrivons-nous* ; where and when do we arrive? Can we even know if we arrive, if arriving ever happens, even comes, if it is only to-come?

For, to drift implies a certain direction one is headed from heading to headed for; without these indicators indications markers points in-relation-with each other one would just be moving.

But, can one know — intend — one's drift?

One who drives who thinks themselves a driver imagines they are a driven-person even as to be driven always also implies being moved-around (hello Ms Daisy), would almost certainly say so. But even as (s)he is starting her slide, all (s)he can know is that she is setting the car, herself, the car with herself in it, in motion ...

... after which, the drift itself takes over.

And, all (s)he can do is: attend to it.

Peut-être l'attente l'oubli.

Where, at the point of the drift, both (s)he and the car are drifting — and here, one might not even be able to separate the movement from the ones involved in it, with it, within it.

Where, without either, there would be no drift; for, there is no drifting without the drifter.

Where, both the drifter and the drifting are in relation — in which, all they can know is that there is a relation.

Where, *the drift itself is relation.*

A *non-essence.*

But, it is not as if we cannot speak of it — after all we are or at least I am trying to.

Perhaps though: we can only speak *as if* we can speak of it. Where, it is always an imaginary gesture; and what is being imagined is the relation between the drift and the one(s) drifting.

Where, what is imagined is nothing other than *the drift* itself, *la dérive elle-même.*

Perhaps then, *what are we drifting from, drifting to?*, is a moot question.

As is, *what is drifting?*

Perhaps then, all we can say is ...

— *la dérive* —

Where, to speak of *drift* is to attempt to speak of the unspeakable.

> *Language is essentially discreet: what it expresses can always also be an instrument of encryption, a means of dissembling, disfiguring, or lying. Since, however, it constitutes all oppositions in the first place, it can belong to none of them, neither to concealment nor disclosure, neither publicity nor privacy and its idiosyncrasies.*
>
> ~ Werner Hamacher[145]

Not that what is speakable and what is unspeakable are antonyms: if that were so,

---

[145] Werner Hamacher, '"Disgregation of the Will": Nietzsche on the Individual and Individuality' in *Premises: Essays on Philosophy & Literature from Kant to Celan*, translated by Peter Fenves, Palo Alto: Stanford University Press, 1999, 173.

speaking the unspeakable would make no sense, be a contradiction. But, that in every act of speaking, something unspeakable is potentially spoken: something that opens, ruptures, wounds even. And not just that — at the point where it punctures, speaking itself moves out of the way for the unspeakable; speaking itself disappears.

Perhaps then, as Jean Baudrillard might say, « the whole art is to know how to disappear before dying, and instead of dying ».[146]

You have to lose your way to find yourself in the right place

~ Gilles Massot[147]

And where *right place* cannot quite be known until one is there — where, at best, one can *sense*, we might even call it *feel*, that (s)he is *right where (s)he belongs*, if only for a moment.

Even if *there*, wherever said place may be, were exactly where (s)he were only a

---

[146] Jean Baudrillard, 'The art of disappearing: an interview with Truls Lie' in *Eurozine* (17 April 2007).

[147] Gilles Massot, *You have to lose your way to find yourself in the right place*, selected works shown at the NUS Museum, 14 June – 31 December 2019.

moment before — even if this feeling disappears, even if (s)he no longer senses the appearance of this feeling only a moment after.

Where *right place* might well be what Alain Badiou calls « an opening of a new world in an old world »,[148] that is *an event*.

Where what is « new » might well be one's own self, a self that « you » could well first have to « lose » ; where the finding might well be *à la recherche du temps perdu*.

To lose: *une ligne de fuite* that might lead one somewhere, might open possibilities for one, might open us up to possibilities in one, might well also leak away, escape from one, slip beneath, fly above you ...

        to lose — to find
        to come — to go

... bearing in mind that a *dash* links both brings together, allows both to touch, whilst always keeping them apart and where to be

---

[148] Alain Badiou described, one might even say *conceives of*, an event in these terms during his seminar, *Philosophy, Ethics, Art*, at The European Graduate School, in August 2004.

dashed is always also to run the risk of being broken into parts.

Dériver / Arrivée : not so much *from where* or *to where*. For, both are not quite any thing, nor have any point, without each other. Where one might even say each one only exists due to the *slash* between them dividing and connecting them, connection only in division — *le trait oblique*.

Where, *to drift away* and *to arrive* are not only in relation to each other, in a relationship with each other, nor merely dependent on the other, but which bear *oblique traces* of each other within.

Slanty.

Perhaps even shadowy.

Where perhaps all I have been attempting to read all I have been trying to write on speak about — all of my attempts to remarks on, make marks about — *Dancing Without Touching*,[149] all my alleged-thoughts touchings on the beautiful work brought

---

[149] Sarah Choo Jing, *Dancing Without Touching*, solo show at Yeo Workshop, 7 January – 26 February 2023.

forth by my dear friend, Sarah Choo Jing,[150] are the illicit markings ghostly remarks spectral marks of what has to remain in the shadows be unseen perhaps unread or read in shadows ... where, *shadow reading* might well be an echo of Socrates and Phaedrus reading in the shadow of trees, relying on it not only for shade but being shady themselves ...

---

[150] Sarah Choo Jing (b. 1990, Singapore) is known for her interdisciplinary approach to photography, video and installation. Her work depicts identifiable moments and characters within contemporary urban society suggesting a plethora of private and often solitary narratives. The artist is concerned with the gaze of the flaneur, voyeurism, and the uncanny.

Choo lives and works in Singapore, since completing her MFA at the Slade School of Art in London in the summer of 2015. Choo recently clinched the 3D Interactive award for The Lumen Prize for Art and Technology 2021; was shortlisted as a Finalist for the Audemars Piguet Art Commission for Art Basel 2020; and was invited to present her practice at Le Brassus, Geneva in Switzerland. She clinched the Gold Award in the 2019 PX3 Prix de la Photographie Competition; the 2017 Perspectives 40 under 40 Award; and came in First Place in the 2015 Moscow International Foto Awards. Choo was also awarded the ICON De Martell Cordon Bleu Photography Award, and the Kwek Leng Joo Prize of Excellence in Still Photography Award in 2013.

She has since exhibited internationally at the Turku Art Museum in Helsinki (2019), National Museum of Singapore (2017), Busan Museum of Art in Korea (2016), Artparis at The Grand Palais in Paris (2015), the START Art Fair at The Saatchi Gallery in London (2015) and Photo London at The Somerset House in London (2015). Her works are collected by both private individuals and public institutions; including the Chrysler Museum of Art, Singapore Art Museum, the National Museum of Singapore, and The Arts Club Permanent Art Collection in London.

Attempting to speak of trying to speak on what cannot be spoken of, of what can only be uttered in-between speech in the silent speech in a *speech*, as Michel Foucault might say, *in a speech which only begins after death* — inter-diction; *interdiction*.

Where, to read is to attempt to touch to feel; perhaps even each other.

Where, to attempt to think — particularly under a shady tree — is to always also open oneself to not only being in the shadows to be accused of hiding sheltering oneself from the law but always also to the possibility of drifting-off.

Dériver —
perchance to dream.

And where one can never quite tell if said thought that comes to one came from one had arrived onto one or if one might have merely drifted to it; into it.

Where the very notion of *having a thought* itself might well only be *thought teasing one*. And where *teasing out a thought* always already opens one self to being teased.

But perhaps we are always only — can only ever be — dancing.

ACT II

And what costume shall the poor girl wear
To all tomorrow's parties?
For Thursday's child is Sunday's clown.
For whom none will go mourning
A blackened shroud, a hand-me-down gown
Of rags and silks, a costume
Fit for one who sits and cries
For all tomorrow's parties.

~ The Velvet Underground[151]

Sarah Choo Jing
Only Nearer Than Half A World Apart
2023
Diasec Print
51 x 150 cm

---

[151] Lou Reed, 'All Tomorrow's Parties' in *The Velvet Underground & Nico*. New York: Verve Records, 1967.

Just wanna dance all night
And I'm all messed up, I'm so out of line,
Stilettos and broken bottles
I'm spinning around in circles
And I'm in the corner, watching you kiss her, oh
And I'm right over here, why can't you see me? Oh
And I'm giving it my all
But I'm not the guy you're taking home, ooh
I keep dancing on my own.

~ Robyn[152]

---

[152] Robyn & Patrick Berger, 'Dancing On My Own' in *Body Talk Pt.1*, Stockholm: Konichiwa Records, 2010.

ACT II sc. ii

Espadas

*Me dijo: "vos sos una chica
que transforma la naturaleza",
y se cortó la comunicación.
Y tuve miedo,
yendo por el medio de la calle,
esquivando a los autos
que venían hacía mí.
Pero como me sentía pura,
seguía caminando,
porque esa era mi prueba de valor.
Las chicas que caminan
solas por la noche son valientes.
Ellas luchan por transformar
su miedo en espadas.*

~ Micaela Piñero[153]

---

[153] Micaela Piñero, 'Espadas' en *Universidad de la violencia*. Buenos Aires: Mansalva, 2018, 23.

Swords

He said to me: « you are a girl
who transforms nature »,
and communication was cut.
And I was afraid,
descending into the middle of the street,
dodging cars
that were coming towards me.
But since I felt pure,
continued to walk,
because it was the test of my courage.
The girls who walk
alone at night they are valiant.
They fight to transform
their fear into swords.

~ Micaela Piñero,
translated by Jeremy Fernando

Every translation signifies the space-between, the gap,
the historical chasm or the repression of history;
translation is the most cautious form of
communication since there is always the inherent
admission of a certain departure and an uncertain
arrival.

~ Hubertus von Amelunxen[154]

---

[154] Hubertus von Amelunxen, 'Afterword' in Vilém Flusser, Towards a Philosophy of Photography, translated by Anthony Matthews, London: Reaktion Books, 2000, 88.

ACT II sc. iii

....-.. .-.. ---

.. .... / - .... . .-. . / .- -. -.-- -... --- -.. -.-- / --- ..- - / - .... . .-. . .

.--. .-.. .- ... . / -.- -. --- -.-. -.- / .. ... . / -.-- --- ..- / -.-. .- -. / .... . .- .-. / -- .

.. .... / - .... . .-. . / .- -. -.-- --- -. . / .- - / .- .-. .-.. .-..

... / ... ..- .--. .--, --- ... . / -. --- -

--- .... / .--. . .-.. .-..

... .. --. ....

[-.-. .- -. / --- -. . / .... . -. / .... .. --. .... / .. -. / -.. .- ... . / .- -. .-.. / -.. --- - ...]

[.- .-. . / - .... . .-. . / .. .-. . .-. . .-.. / -.-. - .. --- -. ...]

-. --- - . ...

.-. . -- .-. .-. --.- ..- . ....

.- .... / - .... . / ,--, --- ... . -... .. .-.. .. - .. . ... / --- ..- . / -- ..- ... .. -.-.

--. ..- . ... / .. .----. .-.. .-.. / -.- . . .--. / -... . -. -.-. .. -. --. / --- -. / -- -.-- / --- .-- -.

-.-- . ... / .. / -.- . . .--. / -... . -. -.-. .. -. --. / --- -. / -- -.-- / --- .-- -.

ACT III

Sarah Choo Jing
Only Nearer Than Half A World Apart
2023
Video Sculpture
63 x 100 x 100 cm

*Que la luz del día ilumine mi corazón,
como el día no lo hizo.
Que la luz del día encienda mi corazón,
como el día no lo hizo.*

~ Micaela Piñero[155]

---

[155] Micaela Piñero, 'Montañas' en *Universidad de la violencia*. Buenos Aires: Mansalva, 2018, 54.

ACT III sc. ii

I love you.

Where everything lies, as Roland Barthes remains to remind us in that characteristically-beautiful way only he can, where « everything is in the speaking of it: it is a 'formula', but this formula corresponds to no ritual; the situations in which I say I-love-you cannot be classified: I-love-you is irrepressible and unforeseeable ... too articulated to be no more than an impulse, too phatic to be a sentence ... It is neither quite what is uttered (no message is congealed, sorted, mummified within it, ready for dissection) nor quite the uttering itself (the subject does not allow himself to be intimidated by the play of interlocutory sites). We might call it a proffering, which has no scientific place: I-love-you belongs neither in the realm of linguistics nor in that of semiology. Its occasion (the point of departure for speaking it) would be, rather, Music. In the manner of what happens in singing, in the proffering of I-love you, desire is neither repressed (as in what is uttered) nor recognised (where we did not expect it: as in the uttering itself) but simply:

released, as an orgasm. Orgasm is not spoken, but it speaks and it says: I-love-you ».[156]

a burst

    a musical burst

        a burst as music

Or, music as burst — music to the point of bursting — music at the point of bursting.

Or, perhaps even:
music as the bursting point.

Which also suggests that the point of love — as least in so far as one can hear its whispers — is also the point where Music bursts, is perhaps the point where it is no longer musical, is the point where it is quite possibly beyond the realm of, *au-delà du ton de la*, musicality ...

untz
untz
untz

---

[156] Roland Barthes. *A Lover's Discourse: Fragments*, translated by Richard Howard. London: Vintage, 2002: 149.

ACT III sc ii

mmm music, a musical thinking, thinking as music, a musicality of thought, a muse that leads us to thinking, thinking which amuses us, that might well leave us all bemused.

smiling — thinking — dancing

> *Nobody puts Baby*
> *in a corner*
>
> ~ Johnny Castle[157]

A certain timbre of thought, as it were.

And here, it might be the moment (but who knows though, one can only hope so) to open our registers to the thought of Jean-Luc Nancy, in particular, to his notes, his notable notations, his notations as notes (so perhaps always a reminder that they have to be played to be heard, to be heard as playful), to his reminder that, « timbre is communication of the incommunicable: provided it is understood that the incommunicable is nothing other, in a

---

[157] Eleanor Bergstein, *Dirty Dancing*, directed by Emile Ardolino. Chicago: Vestron Pictures, 1987.

perfectly logical way, than communication itself, that thing by which a subject makes an echo — of self, of the other, it's all one — it's all one in the plural ».[158]

Moreover, as Nancy continues, « communication is not transmission, but a sharing that becomes subject: sharing as subject of all 'subjects'. An unfolding, a dance, a resonance. Sound in general is first of all communication in this sense. At first it communicates nothing — except itself. At its weakest and least articulated degree, one would call it a noise. (There is noise in the attack and extinction of a sound, and there is noise in sound itself.) But all noise also contains timbre. In a body that opens up and closes at the same time, that arranges itself and exposes itself with others, the noise of its sharing (with itself, with others) resounds: perhaps the cry in which the child is born, perhaps an even older resonance in the belly and from the belly of a mother ».[159]

---

[158] Jean-Luc Nancy. *Listening,* translated by Charlotte Mandell. New York: Fordham University Press, 2007 41.

[159] *ibid*, 41.

An original sound: perhaps even an echo from — dare we say *of* — an origin.

Not that one can have access to this moment: or, even if one did, not that one would/could know, have known, one did. For, even as one speaks, attempts to speak of origins, of an *auctor*, one should try not to forget that one is always already quite possibly authoring altering it.

ACT III sc. iii

On ne voit rien.
On n'entend rien.
Et cependant quelque chose
rayonne en silence ...

- Antoine de Saint-Exupéry[160]

The work of art is not an instrument of
communication. The work of art has nothing to do
with communication. The work of art strictly does
not contain the least bit of information. To the
contrary, there is a fundamental affinity between the
work of art and the act of resistance. There, yes. It
has something to do with information and
communication as acts of resistance. What is this
mysterious relation between a work of art and an act
of resistance when men who resist have neither the
time nor sometimes the necessary culture to have the
least relation to art?

I don't know.

- Gilles Deleuze[161]

But what if the work is housed, is enframed
— behind glass, in between narrow and

---

[160] Antoine de Saint-Exupéry, *Le petit prince*. Stuttgart: Reclams Universal-Bibliothek, 2015, 95.

[161] Gilles Deleuze, Having an Idea in Cinema [On the Cinema of Straub-Huillet], translated by Eleanor Kaufman, in *Deleuze and Guattari: New Mappings in Politics, Philosophy and Culture*, edited by Eleanor Kaufmann and Kevin Jon Heller. Minneapolis: Minnesota University Press, 1998, 18.

partly open passageways along walls; *dans une galerie*, that is, within a gallery?

Sarah Choo Jing
Dancing Without Touching
2022
Gallery Render

For, the moment works are housed, encased, are placed within an *oikos*, they are also withdrawn from the *polis*, from the public; made *private* — all whilst trying not to forget that to be private is also to be made voiceless; to be excluded from citizenry; to be the one that cannot learn; to be an *idiotes*.

Much like when the works are taken (*prendre*) by, taken into, one's grasp — placed under one's conception, one's comprehension.

And, it should weigh on one's mind that the moment one attempts to attend to a work, to works, to address it write on them speak about it — even if one is attempting to open oneself to possibilities, to the works themselves, to the contours the steps the angles of the path the labyrinth that Sarah Choo Jing has laid out for us (where is the Minotaur?; perhaps, as importantly, are there any threads for us to follow?; are they merely red herrings?; why does it always involve murder, at least a death?; oh let me just fly a little too close to the sun) — the moment one tries to comment on, even think about, a work, one is not only tempted to know to understand to make sense of the works one has no choice but to, if only momentarily, bring it under one's own conceptions framework; where, in attending to the video-works images installations — the crafted constellation — of Sarah Choo Jing to the maze which she has made, even as one is remains amazed one might well already be doing nothing but taming it turning them — the individual works themselves, the entire show named *Dancing without Touching*, thoughts on New World (can we ever think about the place the space without also remembering the devastation of the hotel hearing it crumble, a new world that is always already in the rubbles of our memories in our memory as a rubble a pile which came crashing onto me through sound through the sonic waves of a news broadcast whilst I was in the back of a car ostensibly heading for a holiday to a small break from the mad crush that is the school-system in Singapore a schooling that was is certainly seems to want to always be hell-bent on schooling us into schools swimming in the same direction certainly never against the current going anyway the wind blows in a car traveling north of the peninsula at half-past eleven the morning of the ides of March 1986 not quite five hours after driving past the building still enveloped by the darkness and dreams of the previous night now a ruin perhaps emblematic of what happens to dreams in Singapore that stray-away from a neo-liberal wet dream)[162] into information (as I've clearly just done,

---

[162] On 15 March 1986, at around 11:25am, the Lian Yak Building — which housed Hotel New World — collapsed, due to structural defects and poor-quality construction, leaving 33 people dead. It is considered one of the worst disasters in post-war Singapore.

For more, please see Lim Tin Seng, 'Hotel New World Collapse' in *National Library Board — Singapore Infopedia*.

have been doing, can only ever do, despite myself; perhaps all writing is always also to spite myself).

And where, the very moment of response — any attempt at responding-with opening oneself-to another; that is, any attempt to attend to the very space (and possibility) of responsibility — might well be the instant when the, perhaps even any, potential « acts of resistance » in and of the work are muted.

Where the works themselves are lulled into bed, put to sleep.

And where, the very thing that one comes into a gallery for — to look at works, to see the work, perhaps even to expose oneself to the experience we call art — is precisely what carries the works, transports the pieces, away from the very possibility of art itself.

After all, the road to hell is often paved with good intentions.

All while also trying not to forget that every time one writes about something, one not only writes it into being, brings forth the said object, but also writes its context into existence — recontextualising it if one is feeling generous with oneself but really always also decontextualising it into — and with — a new framing that has little maybe even nothing to do with it at all.

Whilst also bearing in mind — even if this will always remain a burden on one — holding onto the fact, that to frame is always also to *potentially accuse* someone of something (s)he might not have done.

to write — to writhe
perchance in dreams

ACT III sc. iv

Sarah Choo Jing
Dancing Without Touching
2023
5-Channel Video Installation
Duration: 7 minute

ACT III sc. v

And, what is it to love across a screen?

Which might well be the question we are facing, the quest that lies right in front of our eyes as we stand before the works (or the work, perhaps you might prefer to think of *Dancing without Touching* as a whole, even though it is impossible to see all of it in a single glance at one look; but when has impossibility ever stopped anyone from dreaming) — the question of: *what does one do with the prophylactic between*?

How to *touch without touching* as it were — bring forth a touchless touch.

Which might well be the question of: *how does one engender the space for the possibility of an immaculate conception.*

Which suggests we might have to attempt to think of a stage, of what is being staged before our eyes, beyond a frame. Doubly-tricky when said staging is taking place through a screen: for, that would entail imagining a screen that is not just a frame even as it frames everything that we see.

And here, we should bear in mind that the screen is always also a mirror.

And try not to forget, not that the screen will ever allow one to, that your face is screened right back at you, that as you are looking at the screen as you are watching the screens you are also watching yourself watch; and being in those small — tight — booths you might well also be hearing yourself hear hearing yourself mutter to yourself as you watch as you respond as you think, thinking yourself hear.

> *Thinking is always*
> *an affair of the ear*
>
> ~ François Noudelmann[163]

Thinking might well be
my affair of the year.

mmm breathless conversation.

To converse — to twirl-with
to dance-alongside another.

---

[163] François Noudelmann, *The Philosopher's Touch: Sartre, Nietzsche, and Barthes at the Piano*, translated by Brian Reilly. New York: Columbia University Press, 2012, 75.

Which means that even as we are attempting to *turn-with* each other (*versare*) even as we are trying to be with (*con-*) others maybe even whilst we are participating in a debate of sorts against (*versus*) another, this is a dance in which all bodies are separated — screened-off — from each other.

Even if this other is our very self.

For a screen both *shows* and *hides away* at exactly the same time. Which means that even as we scan the screen, even as we might be attempting to pay careful attention, enact the closest of readings, what is screened is potentially being screened, screened-off, even as it is put on screen; and perhaps not even by us but by the screen itself in the very act of screening.

That even as we are putting ourselves on, putting ourselves out onto, exposing ourselves to the light of the screen, it is already layering us with sunscreen.

And even as we might be turning-with each other prancing with alleged-thoughts with thoughts that allege which might well be allegations, dancing in screens through screens on-screen, we should try not to

forget Heidegger's reminder that technology only unveils itself, that we only manage to catch a glimpse of its essence, alleged-essence of what he alleges is an essence one of his essential-allegations, in moments when it breaks down: thankfully, as Paul Virilio tries to never let us forget,
each *tekhnē* brings with it its own, its singular, catastrophe, its own down (*kata*) turn (*strephein*) ... dip, if you prefer.

Which would suggest that all hope lies in the potential failures of the screen; in other words, in the potential of the screen itself — when the screen fails to screen, as it were; or even, *when the screen screens itself as screen.*

Which is not to say that it is a situation that can be programmed, planned, instrumentalised: far from it.

Which also means that all we can do is to await the possibility of such a moment, and attend to them as they happen, if they do: all whilst bearing in mind that *waiting* is not passive; far from it. But that it never knows, cannot know, what it is awaiting — otherwise futurial possibilities are always already enframed, limited, by what is expected. Where, if waiting is about the possibility of

an encounter, it is a state in which one waits:
nothing more, and infinitely nothing less.

To wait — to think;
perchance to dream

Perhaps even whilst we are touching screens,
rubbing the screen with our digits.

Opening the possibility that it is our fingers
(*digits*) doing the feeling, walking, seeing,
opening — by touching, caressing — the
screen. A response which comes through the
skin of our fingers; where one, like a surgeon
examining bodies, is attempting to see
through touch, by stroking seeking
searching fumbling around; where one is
performing a dance through seeing without
seeing, as it were; by feel.

And with one's fingers with all of the fingers
in the dance with dancing fingers perhaps
making our languages, our skins, our
screens, *vibrate with an intensity* that brings
forth certain potentials lying within them.

screens — veils
oh to scream sometimes at screens

But like a veil (*un voile*), it sometimes in moments momentarily turns transforms trans-substantiates even into a sail (*une voile*) ... flies away (*s'envoler*) like a thief (*un voleur*) in the night.

And if this sounds like word-play, like merely playing with words, one might take comfort in the words of the great Australian philosophers — Barry, Maurice, and Robin, Gibb — that « it's only words, and words are all I have/ to take your heart away ».[164]

For, as Roland Barthes tries to never let us forget, « language is a skin: I rub my language against the other. It is as if I had words instead of fingers, or fingers at the tip of my words. My language trembles with desire ».[165]

Ah, to rub ...

May the light of the screen illuminate my heart, like the day does not. May the light of the screen light my heart, like the day does not.

---

[164] Barry, Robin, & Maurice Gibb, 'Words', single. London: Polydor Records, 1968.

[165] Roland Barthes. *A Lover's Discourse: Fragments*, 73. (emphasis mine)

... perchance
to dream

on art:
almost a non-manifesto[166]

white on white, translucent landscape, 2020

Art itself is fundamentally useless.

Which is precisely why those in power have always been fearful of it.

---

[166] A version of this piece was first published in *Full Bleed*, Issue 8: Censorship, 2025: 62-65.

Imagine there's no countries
It isn't hard to do
Nothing to kill or die for
And no religion too

~ John Lennon[167]

For, one should try not to forget that the first to be shot are almost always poets, painters, writers. Not because they actually do anything, but that precisely by doing nothing they give — allowing all echoes of *gift* to resound here — they open the space for us to imagine something else, something other.

And by entwining art with use, all that is done is to tie it down to, to shackle it to, the state.

And here, we should try never to forget that we are in a relationship with what we read, what we see, what we stand before. For, even before this encounter happens — prior to the act of encountering — one has to open oneself to the possibility of the encounter, open oneself to the work. Without necessarily knowing what

---

[167] John Lennon, 'Imagine' in *Imagine*. London: Apple Records, 1971.

encountering a work of art itself even is, let alone means.

> *I am fascinated by the possibilities for a deeper stratum of truth, although please don't ask me what I mean by truth, because nobody can answer that one. But, you see, we are creators. What I do is elevate the audience. I'm intensifying facts to such a degree that they start to get the glow of illumination for you. They acquire insight and poetry of an ecstatic nature, like medieval monks.*
>
> *I'm not interested in myself.*
>
> *You should not expose the deepest recesses of your own soul. It doesn't do anyone any good.*
>
> ~ Werner Herzog[168]

Thus, to claim art has a use is to diminish it, to enchain it to value, production, logic, ratio, reason.

It is to do nothing other than to attempt to erase art.

And the gamble taken each time one picks up a book, looks at a painting, watches a film, stands before something that is made,

---

[168] Erik Hedegaard, 'Werner Herzog: the art of being a death-defying, gonzo filmmaking genius' in *Rolling Stone* (23 March, 2017).

created, brought forth, the risk one runs in attempting to attend to a text, is the possibility of *falling* — along with all the potential disasters this entails — of falling *in love*.

Thus, the stake in art is one's very self.

> *The event is in this sense always catastrophic, like the loop of smoke that begins straight before beginning its fine twist: it arrives at the exact place where the trajectory breaks.*
>
> ~ Anne Dufourmantelle[169]

Which might be why Milan Kundera calls it the *unbearable lightness of being*: for, it is the refusal to be grounded, to be pinned down, to be known, that is unbearable, that continually provokes us, challenges us, perhaps even tears us apart.

And, it is perhaps symptomatic that there is a 'crisis' in art whenever states are obsessed about, and with, concocting an identity. For, if art is about openness to the

---

[169] « *L'événement est en ce sens toujours catastrophique, comme la boucle d'une fumée qui commence droite avant d'amorcer sa fine torsion : il arrive à l'endroit exact où la trajectoire se brise* ».

Anne Dufourmantelle, *Éloge du risque*, Paris: Éditions Payot & Rivages, 2011, 185. The translation from the French is mine.

unknown, is about possibilities — it is of the order of difference rather than identification, sameness.

In other words, art is always anti-stasis, *anti-state*.

And more than that, it is always also a challenge to the self, to our selves: it is a call to attend to the possibility of another, of something that is more important than us.

> *'Cause love's such an old fashioned word*
> *And love dares you to care for*
> *The people on the (People on streets) edge of the night*
> *And loves (People on streets) dares you to change our way of*
> *Caring about ourselves.*
> *This is our last dance*
> *This is our last dance*
> *This is ourselves*
> *Under Pressure*
>
> ~ Queen & David Bowie[170]

And like any call, might well lead us to dash ourselves on the rocks.

Herein lies its danger.

---

[170] Roger Taylor, Freddie Mercury, David Bowie, John Deacon, and Brian May, 'Under Pressure' in Queen, *Hot Space*. Santa Fe: Elektra Records, 1982.

And its beauty.

You may say I'm a dreamer
But I'm not the only one
I hope some day you'll join us
...

the curator
for Sylvère Lotringer[171]

I

Sylvère Lotringer at The European Graduate School, June 2016

A figure, in the precise sense of one who cares (*cura*) for — books, works, texts, people, ideas, people, oh people —, one might even say a guardian of ideas and people, persons with ideas, is no longer with us ...

---

[171] A version of this work was first published as the 27th edition of *One Imperative* in December 2023.

Most everywhere else, they have already been swallowed by the rise of the salesperson. Or *the gallerist*, if you prefer the other name with which they go by. And here, it is not too difficult to hear echoes of Sylvère and Jean Baudrillard, both of whom continue to teach us that *use-value* is a misnomer: for, the value of something lies in it being exchanged, in its exchangeability, is premised on, can only be generated through, exchange. Thus, *exchange-value* is tautological. One might even say that the term *use-value* attempts to maintain the notion, even illusion, that materiality has an inherent value, that there is a 'proper use' for something — and, in that way, is an attempt to hold on to the fantasy of a means of production where exchange is not an abstraction; where we are not alienated, always already separated, from that production. And stave-off the fact that our relationship with materials, with the world, with any and every other — even if it involves production — is always already mired in exchange, in valuation, in consumption.

In movement — ideally with a maximal circulation, at the highest acceleration

possible: and, as Sylvère's old friend, Paul
Virilio, continues to teach us, « the faster you
go, the farther you have to look, and you
lose lateral vision. You are fascinated ... From
now on everything will happen without our
even moving, without our even having to set
out ».[172]

> *No wonder art history has recently achieved a new visibility.*
> *The more blurred the boundaries, the more necessary it becomes*
> *to keep everything in its proper place.*[173]

Which is no fault of the gallerist as such:
after all they are merely living up to their
call to *play to the gallery*.

And, it is perhaps of no coincidence that
galleries quite possibly bring with them
echoes of church porches (*galilea*), albeit
from afar (which might well be apt seeing
that a *portico* is part of its structure) — after
which, the *klang of coins* is never far behind ...

... render unto Caesar.

---

[172] Paul Virilio, interview with Caroline Dumocel, translated by Pauline Eiferman, in 'The Catastrophes Issue', *VICE Magazine*, September 2010.

[173] Sylvère Lotringer, in an interview with Jean Baudrillard, 'Too Much is Too Much' (2001) in *The Conspiracy of Art*, translated by Ames Hodges, Los Angeles: Semiotext(e), 2005, 80.

Curatorial language is the language of people who are afraid of not having ideas.[174]

Perhaps though, as Jean Baudrillard remains to continue to remind us, « the whole art is in knowing how to disappear before dying and instead of dying ».[175] For in disappearing, one plays the final trick — might get to have the last laugh, as it were — not by returning, resurrecting, but by completely vanishing.

Even more so when something has gone well: for, *whenever there is a model it's going to be duplicated and then it becomes an industry.*[176] And, « as soon as a programme is presented », Michel Foucault adds (or, one is tempted to say 'intervenes', so why not,

---

[174] This notion, amongst many others, was explored by Sylvère as part of his seminar — *Jean Baudrillard* — at The European Graduate School in June 2016.

[175] Jean Baudrillard, *Why Hasn't Everything Already Disappeared?*, translated by Chris Turner, with images by Alain Willaume, Calcutta: Seagull Books, 2009, 25.

[176] Sylvère, in conversation with Jack Smith, 'Uncle Fishhook and the Sacred Baby Poo Poo of Art' in 'Schizo-culture', *Semiotext(e)* magazine, edited by Sylvère Lotringer, 1976, & in *Hatred of Capitalism: a Semiotext(e) reader*, edited by Chris Kraus and Sylvère Lotringer, Los Angeles: Semiotext(e), 2001, 255.

intervenes) « it becomes a law and there's a prohibition against inventing ».[177]

Thankfully, *once you've realised what everything is and how it works, how it's going to repeat itself, endlessly, you just step out of it, and affirm other, positive values*.[178] « I do not want to accuse; I do not even want to accuse those who accuse » — the Nietzschean echo begins (and here, we should try not to forget that almost everyone on the pages of this chapter considers themselves a follower of the very one who warns us of following) — « Looking away shall be my only negation. And all in all and on the whole: some day I wish to be only a Yes-sayer ».[179]

However, as Nietzsche also warns us, one should always be wary of one's disciples (so, also followers). For the « yes » of affirmation has nothing to do with yes-men; affirming life, saying « yes » to life, generating, creating, has naught to do with

---

[177] Michel Foucault, 'Friendship as a Way of Life', translated by John Johnston, in *Foucault Live: Collected Interviews, 1961-1984*, Los Angeles: Semiotext(e)—Double Agents Series, 1989, 312.

[178] 'Uncle Fishhook and the Sacred Baby Poo Poo of Art', 257.

[179] Friedrich Nietzsche, *The Gay Science*, section 276, translated with commentary by Walter Kaufmann, New York: Vintage Books, 1974, 223.

agreeing-with, even less so with being an agreeable sycophant.

Nor with disciplines, which do nothing other than programatise (quite often under the banner of pragmatisation): *it's order that has become criminal, abnormal ...*[180]

Or, even worse, aligning oneself with, saying « yes » to, positive-sounding terms, like *humanism* for instance: *maybe we're not conscious enough of the inhumanity of the idea of humanity presented to us ... the inhumanity of the kind of civilisation we're trying to produce ... if you can call civilisation this craze for worldwide annihilation.*[181]

However, and here we return to Paul Virilio once again (whether we are conversing with him or interjecting into the conversation with Caroline Dumocel here is yet another question, perhaps not entirely unrelated though; maybe always between-holdings, *entretien*), « choosing resistance is not opposing yourself to new technologies, but

---

[180] Sylvère, in conversation with Jacques Latrémolière, 'I talked with God about Antonin Artaud' in Sylvère Lotringer, *Mad Like Artaud*, translated by Joanna Spinks, Minneapolis: Univocal Publishing, 2015, 74.

[181] *ibid*, 70.

refusing to collaborate ».¹⁸² For, to resist is to attune oneself to the resisting possibilities in each *tekhnē*, to the possibilities of resistance brought forth in each technology — all while trying to remain aware (insofar as this is even or ever possible) of its potential catastrophes, « refusing to collaborate » with its programmatic designations where possible; *I see it as a complete refusal to compromise*;¹⁸³ perhaps by « looking away », turning (*strephein*) away, even down (*kata*); whilst remaining open to the possibility that there are happy-accidents; recognising them, listening to them, hearing *a resonance, a source of resonance from that huge rupture*.¹⁸⁴ For, it is not about refusing to make books because books have also become mere objects of exchange; but, instead, bringing forth texts that refuse to be put-to-work (*labore*) in the same way as the rest of the shiny-shiny, are even-whilst-small too-big to be bite-sized, cannot be shelved-away, placed on display, shoved aside, easily palatable, resolutely remain uncomfortably unconsumable. So, books like « my books » which, as Hélène Cixous says, « do not settle

---

[182] Paul Virilio, interview with Caroline Dumocel.

[183] 'I talked with God about Antonin Artaud', 72.

[184] *ibid*, 69.

down. I like books that slip away, the escapees ».[185] *Perhaps if one listens to oneself, one starts to hear better.*[186]

---

[185] Hélène Cixous, interview with Rosalind C. Morris, 'The Writing, Always the Writing', translated by Keith Cohen and Eric Nowitz, in *French Intelligence*, edited by Sylvère Lotringer, Los Angeles: Semiotext(e)—Double Agents Series, 2002, & in *Hatred of Capitalism*, 123.

[186] 'I talked with God about Antonin Artaud', 72.

II

Mark Von Schlegell   *What do you want it* to be?*

Chris Kraus   *I want it to be beautiful.*[187]

//

Sylvère Lotringer   *When I was doing a lot of interviews it was because I wanted theory to become ideas, that would have a direct impact. That would be grasped as naturally as you breathe.*

Chris Kraus   *Conversational theory.*

Sylvère Lotringer   *Yeah. Interviews were one way to do it. The other was to surround it with other stuff, 'til it became part of something more fluid and couldn't be isolated. Documents, images, quotes, ideas being part of some kind of movement that takes you from one thing to the next, and changes*

---

[187] Chris Kraus in conversation with Sylvère Lotringer, 'The History of Semiotext(e)' in *Hatred of Capitalism*, 16.

everything about the world.[188]

//

Chris Kraus   ... *it's more like an atmosphere of meaning than any particular meaning ...*[189]

[*it here being *Hatred of Capitalism* which Mark Von Schlegell had edited sections of]

Which might well be why the magazine — consciously or otherwise, can one really ever tell the difference; we might all well be *mad like Artaud* — was first named so: « I looked through your magazine and I was repelled by the title, *Semiotext(e)*. It's so dry, you just want to throw it in the trash, which I did. Listen: *Hatred of Capitalism* would be a much better title. It's stunning. The world is starving for thoughts. If you can think of something, the language will fall into place, but the thought is what's going to do it ».[190]

One can well imagine Sylvère chuckling upon hearing this. Chuckling, as Hannah

---

[188] *ibid*, 16.

[189] *ibid*, 20.

[190] epigraph to *Hatred of Capitalism*.

Arendt, the one who you really couldn't imagine chuckling all that much — but what do I know; can you really tell anything about anyone from their writing, their work ('your work being your life', being one of the great, if not one of the greatest, lies of capitalism) — teaches us, hopefully whilst chuckling, « the greatest enemy of authority is contempt, and the surest way to undermine it is laughter ».[191]

And then going on, alongside Chris, playing along with Jack's idea to name the '2001 Semiotext(e) reader' as such, in fact foregrounding it in the epigraph: not because it would capture more attention, increase sales, or any such thing — nothing that banal — but in *memory of an era (1974 – 2002)*;[192] not as some act of nostalgia, for this is a dedication to an « era » extending past the time of the collection, to a certain future that perhaps can only be glimpsed through the past. For, even as the time in which all of these pieces have been written has passed, it is not as if *the time of the texts themselves* have: *capitalism hasn't disappeared. Its repercussions*

---

[191] Hannah Arendt, *On Violence*, New York: Harcourt Brace & Co., 1969, 45.

[192] dedication, *Hatred of Capitalism*.

are even more momentous than before, but no one can seem to grasp them.[193]

> *What happened is that we forgot that capitalism even exists. It has become invisible because there's nothing else to see.*[194]

> *Perhaps if one listens to oneself, one starts to hear better.*[195]

« Underneath all reason lies delirium, drift », says Gilles Deleuze in conversation with Félix Guattari (in an inscribed conversation so who will ever know which of them said so, just that it was ascribed to GD instead of FG; so it could well also be that both of them, or neither did), « everything is rational in capitalism, except capital or capitalism itself ... it is completely delirious, it is mad. In this sense we say: the rational is always the rationality of an irrational ».[196] *That's what Dada began questioning: logic, dialogic,*

---

[193] 'The History of Semiotext(e)', 16.

[194] *ibid*, 15.

[195] 'I talked with God about Antonin Artaud', 72.

[196] Gilles Deleuze & Félix Guattari, 'Capitalism: A Very Special Delirium' in Félix Guattari, *Chaosophy*, Los Angeles: Semiotext(e) — Foreign Agents Series, 2002, & in *Hatred of Capitalism*, 215.

rational thought — these processes that allow one to speed through without truly grasping things.[197]

This book is like a homing head, finding issues that are urgent in the midst of this diffusion.[198]

Something Sylvère clearly not only understood but embraced: who else would have made, would bring forth, books that were so unique in their singularity and then ensured that they looked pretty much exactly the same, except one who realised that not only are things *same same but different*, but it is only in recognising the repeated sameness that difference is brought forth — that same has to happen twice for it to generate difference. *Literature is like putting on glasses. I see the world differently ... I'm able to see things that would otherwise remain invisible.*[199] That things are not in themselves different, but in being with each other, alongside another — in relation — engender differences: *to surround it with other*

---

[197] 'I talked with God about Antonin Artaud', 79.

[198] 'The History of Semiotext(e)', 20.

[199] 'I talked with God about Antonin Artaud', 82.

stuff, 'til it became part of something more fluid and couldn't be isolated.[200]

That it is not in tragedy but in farce that resistances lie.

Chuckle.

One has to be mad enough to do so. *Why can we accept certain things about Druids, and consider their beliefs legitimate — but when someone takes himself for a Druid and 'becomes' a Druid, we lock him away? If that's madness, then doesn't madness teach us about our own history? About who we are?*[201] And, perhaps as crucially, « not just anyone can go mad ».[202] Oh Lacan ...

Tee hee hee ...

For, to think is quite possibly to do nothing but *to be done with the judgement of God.*

---

[200] 'The History of Semiotext(e)', 16.

[201] 'I talked with God about Antonin Artaud', 78.

[202] epigraph to *Mad Like Artaud*.

Our society desperately needs monsters to reclaim its own moral virginity.[203]

With all of the risks it entails.

When I started Semiotext(e) in 1974 we were in the last gasp of Marxism, and I knew the terrorists were right, but I could not condone their actions. That is still the way I feel right now.[204] « One knows nothing about terrorism if one does not see that it is not a question of real violence, nor of opposing one violence to another (all *real* violence, like real order in general, is always on the side of power) but to oppose the *full* violence and to the *full* order a clearly superior model of extermination and virulence operating through emptiness ». Where, Baudrillard continues, « the secret is to oppose the order of the real, an absolutely imaginary realm, completely ineffectual at the level of reality, but whose implosive energy absorbs everything real and all the violence of the real power which founders there ... A

---

[203] Sylvère in conversation with Johnny, quoted in David Wojnarowicz, 'The Suicide Of A Guy Who Once Built An Elaborate Shrine Over A Mouse Hole' in *Close To The Knives: A Memoir Of Disintegration*, with an introduction by Olivia Laing, Edinburgh: Cannongate Books, 2016, 202.

[204] 'The History of Semiotext(e)', 15.

challenge that is symbolic *before becoming real* ... ».²⁰⁵

*Ahh chérie ...
you always have to pay
for the symbolic ...*²⁰⁶

And Sylvère's challenge — to the university; to so-called intellectuals hiding behind desks, ossified podiums, increasingly rarefied spaces, within institutions; to the, quote-unquote, 'art world'; to the attempted commodification of thought and continual attempts to commodify anything and every thing — was to offer a kind of protection, a shelter, a space: *it was people moving around doing their things and I was just trying to do mine and it didn't matter if it went anywhere or not ... You don't always have to try to make a point.*²⁰⁷ Nor have to subsume every decision under a ratio, reason; as Chris Kraus tells us, « a lot of the people that we publish were

---

²⁰⁵ Jean Baudrillard, 'Our Theatre of Cruelty', translated by John Johnston, in 'The German Issue', *Semiotext(e)* magazine, edited by Sylvère Lotringer, 1982, & in *Hatred of Capitalism*, 54.

²⁰⁶ uttered by Jerome, a character inspired by Sylvère, in Chris Kraus, *Torpor*, London: Tuskar Rock Press, 2017, 103.

²⁰⁷ 'The History of Semiotext(e)', 14.

crazy »;[208] *the Madness of Truth*.[209] A challenge in which *all the books looked almost exactly the same*, « completely ineffectual at the level of reality » — a challenge to the very imagination of capital, bearing in mind that the condition of exchange is differentiation, that one object is differentiable from another. The very same condition that the police need: that it is YOU and not another who did it — *identify yourself! Point that person out! Raise your hand! Stand out from the crowd!* Even to the extent of fabricating a difference where there is none.

And, in doing so, offering shelter — to writers, thinkers, artists; to all who were considered, who might well have been, mad. Sylvère, who would cover us, shade us, offer us the protection of the shadows; all while saying so, admitting to it, openly signing-off to the fact that he was indeed our friend of the woods (*silvestris*).

So, always already hiding in plain sight.

Like the very best kind of password. Secrets: « the sacred », Georges Bataille reminds us,

---

[208] *ibid*, 17.

[209] *ibid*, 17.

being « nothing more than a privileged moment of unity in communion, a convulsive moment full of what is normally smothered ».²¹⁰ The type that can sometimes be found in *little black books*.

With a smile, his sly almost shy smile: not because 'everything will be better' (he is no naïve optimist) nor that 'things can always be worse' (resigned nihilism would be too easy) but with an *optimistic nihilism*: *repression, actually, is an ongoing creation ...*²¹¹

> *Forgetting does not lack anything.*
> *It even becomes assertive, or affirmative ...*²¹²

> *There are so many rulers now.*
> *Authority is everywhere. I could do with*
> *a little more chaos myself ...*²¹³

For maybe, *to care* is to get out of the way, so the works, words, thoughts, ideas, people,

---

²¹⁰ Georges Bataille, 'The Culprit', translated by Tom Gora, 'Polysexuality', *Semiotext(e)* magazine, edited by François Peraldi, 1981, & in *Hatred of Capitalism*, 110.

²¹¹ Sylvère Lotringer, 'The Dance of Signs', translated by Daniel Moshenberg, in 'Nietzsche's Return', *Semiotext(e)* magazine, edited by Sylvère Lotringer, 1978, & in *Hatred of Capitalism*, 177.

²¹² *ibid*, 178.

²¹³ 'Uncle Fishhook and the Sacred Baby Poo Poo of Art', 256.

can speak for themselves. *I was trying to disappear for years by doing interviews.*[214]

Where to disappear is always also to *diss appearance* itself.

> *One does not dream anymore;*
> *One is dreamed of, silence*
>
> ~ Henri Michaux[215]

---

[214] 'The History of Semiotext(e)', 16.

[215] Henri Michaux, 'La Ralentie', as quoted in Paul Virilio, 'The Last Vehicle', in *Looking Back at the End of the World*, edited by Dietmar Kamper and Christoph Wulf, Los Angeles: Semiotext(e)—Foreign Agents Series, 1986, & in *Hatred of Capitalism*, 159.

III

« At any rate », Baudrillard tries to never let us forget, « nothing just vanishes; of everything that disappears there remain traces ».[216] So perhaps the question is not just *what has Sylvère left us?*: that is more straightforward — his teachings, writings, books that he has made, been a part of, people he has taught, inspired, ideas he has unleashed that are so much part of the world that they are *grasped as naturally as you breathe*,[217] all that he has curated, cared for; but, rather — or perhaps more accurately, *also* — what remains that we have not-yet-quite-noticed, that we think are not-there, future-possibilities in the precise sense of pasts-which-have-not-quite-yet-happened.

Perhaps the fact that we are still — I certainly am — continuing to ask this question suggests that he has taken up the suggestion of his old friend, understood it, heard him, better than any of us:

---

[216] Jean Baudrillard, *Why Hasn't Everything Already Disappeared?*, 25.

[217] 'The History of Semiotext(e)', 16.

« disappearing should be an art form, a seductive way of leaving the world. I believe that part of disappearing is to disappear before you die, to disappear before you have run dry, while you still have something to say ... »[218]

So, despite wanting the dance of signs to continue, perhaps indefinitely, I am probably better off going: *I will, here and now, stop wanting the story to go somewhere. I will forget what I know feebly, in advance, in order to gather the whole complexity of forces at play. I will learn to resist the melody of casual relations and the torpor of narrative accumulations in order to reinvent the intensity of risks, ceaselessly menacing and forever being reborn.*[219]

For, it's not about some *telos*, some known end point — *it's preposterous to think there could be any kind of ending or conclusion*[220] — nor about defining, declaring, some metaphysical notion of a life, a life's work, even less so 'what life is' — « I think », the 'I' here being Félix Guattari (whom I think

---

[218] Jean Baudrillard, in conversation with Truls Lie, 'The Art of Disappearing' in *Eurozine*, April 2007.

[219] 'The Dance of Signs', 176.

[220] 'The History of Semiotext(e)', 18.

would appreciate, certainly hope would chuckle at, the scare-quotes around the personal pronoun), « I think it's important to destroy 'big' notions »[221] (like the 'I'; perhaps we should try to forget definite articles) — nor is it about being on some path, journey, launching path to life, but lies in realising one is always already *in life*: « life », as the other Chris, Marker this time, tells us (with a smile on his face, I'd like to believe) « life, to be eaten on the spot, like fresh donuts. It's a very simple secret ... ».[222]

Sometimes, I catch myself wondering if thinkers who posit that *beauty* and *truth* are one and the same thing, or at least can be found in the same realms, were wondering if *moments of truth* (or even glimpses of truth) come, *the Madness of Truth*[223] comes, to us not just through but *as* moments of beauty. That *glimpses of truth* come to us at the very moment when we are *moved beyond ourselves*,

---

[221] Félix Guattari, 'Becoming-Woman', by Rachel McComas and Stamos Metzidakis, in *Soft Subversions*, edited by Sylvère Lotringer, Los Angeles: Semiotext(e) — Foreign Agents Series, 1996, & in *Hatred of Capitalism*, 357.

[222] Chris Marker, 'Sunless' in 'Oasis', *Semiotext(e)* magazine, edited by Brigette Vial, Tim Simone, Martin Avillez, et al., 1984, & in *Hatred of Capitalism*, 323.

[223] 'The History of Semiotext(e)', 17.

when we are, at least momentarily, no longer quite ourselves, that *truth* is a moment that comes, as Berlin (the space, place, of so much madness, but this time the band) sings, to « take my breath away ».[224]

> *Forget meaning and with it the subject.*
> *Beauty will be amnesiac or will not be at all.*[225]

Perhaps I should ... too ...

Tee hee

---

[224] Giorgio Moroder & Tom Whitlock, 'Take My Breath Away' in Berlin, *Radar Radio*, B-side. New York: Columbia Records, 1986.

[225] 'The Dance of Signs', 189.

eating being well
— *shaping space for hospitalities* —[226]

fish, 2019

To eat, perchance to dream,
'aye, there's the rub.

For, to eat is to always *eat-with*, even when you are alone. Where, each dish and every meal contains within it *a multitude of tales:* journeys, travels, histories, images, stains, marks-made, remarks, *les remarques*, notes, notations, music, tones, rhythms,

---

[226] A version of this paper was first presented at the *Shaping Gastronomy* congress, organised by The International Society for Gastronomic Sciences and Studies at L'università di Scienze Gastronomiche di Pollenzo, 26 – 28 September, 2024.

improvisations ... all waiting to be told, heard, seen, felt, touched, tasted.

If only we take the time to see, to hear, to listen, to learn.

And, each time we eat, we are eating not just in but *as* communion; a corporeal coming-together of materials — bodies, ingredients, meats, produce, fishes, crustaceans, herbs, spices, oils, condiments, flavours; gatherings of chefs, suppliers, packers, delivery drivers, farmers, fishermen, cultivators, carpenters, waiters, bartenders, herbalists, horticulturalists, goatherds, cleaners, kitchen assistants, potters, ceramists, artisans who make the very plates from which you are eating — a conference, and sometimes confluence but not always, a conferring of matter (and this matters, not just in the fact that there is new matter brought forth into the world, and that materials have been used to make those works — thus, possibly depriving others of said resources — but that what is made has effects, that *works affect*, leave *traces in the world*; whether we see them, have yet the ability to recognise them, is a related and entirely different question), so yes, a symposia of matter, matterings, and relationships, with their — and your — memories, inscriptions, imaginations, dreams, forgettings.

> *We drink — be it alcohol, caffeine, or water — to slip into our own skin. When we drink, we seek to become more of ourselves, to modify and alter our chemistry; it is an act of solvency, to absolve, to solve, to find a solution. We drink to dilute and concentrate in response to the world around us.*
>
> ~ Sara Chong[227]

Of *beings-with* and *being-withs* that are simultaneously both material and — which momentarily, at least potentially — transcends the profane: where, with each bite, ingestion, consumption, one might always also be taking-in, carrying (*gest*), gestating, whispers of *do this in memory of me*.

And, when you swallow, what of the world comes into you? In ingesting, consuming, taking into you, does it also become part of you? Perhaps even in that quite literal version of, « tell me what you eat and I'll tell you who you are ».[228]

---

[227] Epigraph in Jeremy Fernando & Sara Chong, *Dinner for One: recipes | paintings | photographs | tales*. Tachikawa: Bunker Press, 2023.

[228] Jean Anthelme Brillat-Savarin, Aphorism IV in *The Physiology of Taste*, translated by Anne Drayton. London: Penguin Classics, 1994, 13.

Where, to chew something is always also to *chew on it.*

A taste. A thought.
The taste of thought.

And as Italo Calvino reminds us, each time we chew, there is an « extraction of vital juices », after which a « process of ingestion and digestion leaves its imprint » ; as in « every amorous relationship ».[229] Oh, there might well be love involved. Much like how *a kiss,* as Georges Bataille tries to never let us forget, « *un baiser est le début du cannibalisme* ».[230]

To eat ... to touch ... to kiss ... to know. Where what we ingest *shapes us,* takes us on turns, slants us, informs us, forms us, makes us, in coming to us *becomes us.* Where tears in the batter of a wedding cake not only causes us to cry, tears us up, maybe even tears us

---

[229] Italo Calvino, 'Under the Jaguar Sun', translated by William Weaver, in *Under the Jaguar Sun.* London: Penguin Books, 2013, 27.

[230] Georges Bataille, *L'Érotisme*, Paris, Éditions de Minuit, 1957; as read in Coline Fournier, '« What are you hungry for? » Le cannibalisme dans *Grave* de Julia Ducournau (2016)' in *Érudit*, 12 August 2024: https://www.erudit.org/fr/revues/musemedusa/2023-n11-musemedusa 09504/1112992ar/

apart, but that at that moment of ingestion, of chewing, of eating, we — momentarily — become rivulets flowing down a cheek.

Métamorphose involontaire.

Where in each meal lies a potential *immanent-transcendence.*

But, even as we open ourselves to the possible notions, ideas, even ideals, which reside in these coming-togethers, even as we tune ourselves to listening-to, to attempting to *hear*, the possibilities in these encounters we call *meals*, we should also bear in mind — and carry this burden with us — that there is a *here* to this being-with, this companionship; that breaking bread (*panis*) with (*com-*) happens in a space, a place, the room, the table at which we are seated, the floor under the skies on which we perch ourselves (skies that might have opened themselves to the sun gently warming us, or blistering us; or rain gently refreshing us, or pouring down on us; or filled with bombs raining onto us), the *mesa* at which we congregate, and the peoples whom we eat-with, whom we choose to sit-beside, that we are sometimes put-together-with, that on occasion we are forced to consume alongside, perhaps purely for material sustenance, to survive; that there is a spatial-materiality — of *wheres* and *whats* — to eating, to meals, to living itself.

Which is not at all to say that eating to stay alive is any less, makes one any lesser, than eating well: for not only is the latter premised on the former, in a world in which so many are deprived, lack basic sustenance, denigrating survival would be obscene, disgusting really, and should leave a bad taste in one's mouth. It would be an inhospitability — effacing the possibility of *hospice, hôpital, cura*, care, itself.

However, one might posit that *eating well,* eating *as a way of living, of life*, is even riskier: for, if *living well* entails opening oneself to the meal, to others, to possibilities, then it always also is an opening to the possibilities of *contamination.*

All of which can sometimes bring our ideals back, if not crashing, down to earth, certainly severely limiting them, perhaps framing them (even accusing them of something they might not have done), certainly shaping, sometimes un-shaping, often re-shaping, them.

Which is not to say that just because we seem to be in the same place that every meal is the same. For, each *coming-together* occurs at a specific site: there is *a singularity* to touch. And not only is it that « one never steps in the same river twice », as Heraclitus continues to teach us, albeit fragmentarily (how do fragments shape themselves to each other; what is the shape of the entire piece, if there is such a thing as a whole; are wholes this hole that have a hold on us?), but — as importantly — that « things, they keep their secrets ».[231]

To step, to try to cross, step across, to potentially step over, side step maybe, sometimes step on.

And, as importantly, that each moment of touch takes-place on a threshold: occurs on a border, boundary, *limine*, in the *skin-between*.[232] So, always also involving immigrations, emigrations, invitations, warmth, welcome, generosities, negotiations,

---

[231] Heraclitus, *Fragments*, translated by Brooks Haxton with a foreword by James Hilman (London: Penguin Classics, 2003).

[232] And here, one might also — as perhaps my old teacher, Siegfried Zielenski, might — open the register that the skin-between, the *simulacrum*, is precisely the site in which Lucretius posits lies the space, and possibility, of communication.

skirmishes, resistances, evictions, policings, declarations of strangeness, strangers, *xenoi*.

Where, what is at stake is nothing less than the relationship between a host and their guest.

Alongside the question of *what turns a host into a kidnapper?*; and its compendium, *at what point does a guest transform into an invader?*. Bringing with it the perennial question *who gets to decide?* : is it the guest who determines whether the host were a good one; is the host the one who ultimately judges whether you were gracious, or a pain-in-the-ass. And is there such a thing as being inherently hospitable? ; where you — regardless of the role you were playing, maybe even what you did — were being unappreciated, perhaps even misunderstood.

Which will then bring with it the question: *are you a hospitable person?*, or *a person who was being hospitable at that moment in time?* Which is also the question of: *is hospitality ontological or does it lie in immanence?*[233]

---

[233] And, as my old friend Hamant Singh reminds us, « at what point does one overstay their welcome as a guest? This would simultaneously depend on not the guest or the host but the interaction between them. That a guest could behave exactly the same as he does with one host

Alongside, what might be the implications of calling it a 'hospitality industrial': certainly we have industrialised it (it has long already been militarised; the most apparent example being the kitchen brigade system, with its structures and hierarchies); which is not to say it is not useful, far from it. But it is certainly a commodification of a relationship, where the *mode* which takes precedence is, its *modalities* are, that of production. And whenever we have modes, they always also bring with them measurements, exactitudes, extractions, exemptions, expulsions — manners of acting and doing in which *appropriate measures* are supposed to be taken — valuations, values, exchanges ... along with their fashions, so always subject to whims, arbitrary judgements, decisions, laudation, ribbons, stars, condemnations, ruinations, closures.

The matterings of matter.

---

and be within the limits of being hosted and yet overstay his welcome with another host ».

Or even with the same host: with the same interaction (if that were possible) being conceived as appropriate, even good, at one time, and not another.

Where both, all, sides always have a role to play, but where it is also — at the same time — not totally in any one's hands.

Keeping in mind that whatever decision is made, whichever judgement is passed on one, it is not one just involving *praxis,* but is potentially on one's very being.

And whenever the dossier of decisions, of making decisions — so always also a question of *choice,* of *choosings,* of *volition* — is opened, it once again brings with it the accompanying questions of *who gets to choose, who gets to decide,* along with its slightly more sinister relative, *whose matterings matter more?*

Which is no surprise since the question of hospitality, and hospitality as a quest, has been with us ever since a stranger appeared on our doorsteps, on the threshold of our homes — our *oikos,* so always already bringing with it concerns of norms, *nomos,* and the economy — the moment, and every time, someone comes to us requesting sustenance, safety, shelter, sometimes even a measure of management, of guidance, or even rules, And here, one should always pay homage to the space in which we are in, to our hosts to which we try to be good guests (thus bringing with it the question of *is writing a form of hosting?* or is the writer a guest being hosted by the ones who read, who can turn throw you out the door in an instant if one isn't deemed good enough, if one is now deemed to be invading their space; and if writing is hosting, then the one who writes must ensure that it doesn't — in this case, I don't — turn *from host to kidnapper*, where you are being held hostage).

Where *being hospitable* is nothing more and infinitely nothing less than a practice of *giving shape to* relationships; residing — created and constantly recreated — in each, and as a result of, every decision and choice made. And here, one should try not to forget that practices form habits, which in turn give shape to our *habitus*; both in terms of our bodies and our selves, one might even say, our beings.

After all, *being, eating, being hospitable*, are all verbs, doings, makings, bodily makings which are quite possibly making bodies. And where *being well* and *eating well* are intertwined, perhaps even indivorceable from each other, while never also being reducible to each other —

and their borders
quite possibly rather porous.

Whether one is cognisant, can ever be fully aware, of the effects of these decisions being quite another question. Perhaps this be where the threshold between accountability and responsibility lie: and if you are hearing echoes of limits, borders, possible encounters, again, it wouldn't just be voices in your head.

And, perhaps above all (if you allow a touch of irony that *Aufhebung* might be resounding here), where neither *being* nor *eating* are solely ideas, nor should remain in the realm of ideals: they are both practices, and should be practised, honed, continuously ... and with, and alongside, others.

Moreover, if one only looks at the stars, you might well fall into a well.

So, perhaps the question we are left with is: *how might we give shape to that space, that place — that encounter — we call eating, being, with?*

Which might be particularly pertinent to us all here who constantly put ourselves under judgment — whether we are chefs, growers, nurturers of the land, whether we open doors for others, sometimes literally, sometimes as teachers, as people who take on apprentices, who lay tables, who set up welcomes for people, who write on, think about, make works speaking to, these question, who send ourselves on quests to respond to the questions, who allow these questions (willingly or otherwise) to send us on journeys, adventures, sometimes involving hijinks, often onto unknown paths, almost certainly where the *hodos* remains veiled from any possible *meta* — who are constantly called upon, sometimes called out, who have somewhat willingly submitted ourselves to this masochistic contract of being put before the law, even if the gates leading to this law (ah, yet another threshold), even if *le portail*, might be of our own making.

And should one ever raise a complaint, one is told that *this is the path that you have chosen*, that you have to *walk the walk*, that it is *their way or the highway*.

But still, regardless of the trials that one might be facing on one's walks, one must also bear in mind that even as one is able to walk, to move around, to roam, there are many who can no longer walk, who no longer feel safe to walk, who are not allowed to walk. From much maligned indentured workers, whose walk, whose movement, is seen, constantly construed — vindictively, racially, perhaps even stupidly — as a threat; to civil-rights marches that are cordoned, shepherded, uncivilly beaten, violently attacked; to assemblies — in Buenos Aires, Budapest, Bangkok, Caracas, Mexico City, Mariupol, Oakland, Lampedusa, Kiev, Hong Kong, Taipei, Rio, Warsaw, Kuala Lumpur, Seoul, Gaza, oh Gaza, amongst many many others, sometimes invisible ones, like in Moscow, Beijing, Pyongyang, Singapore — that are threatened, charged upon, brutally dispersed in order to make way for certain kinds of movements that are authorised, approved, sanctioned; to our lesbian, gay, bi-sexual, trans-gender, queer, intersex, asexual, friends whose drives, desires, tastes, bodies, are policed, criminalised, who are told to get behind, keep themselves concealed behind, closed doors, closets, unable to walk in the open, to waltz in the sun, who are told that their attractions, their bodily passions, are beyond the pale; whose very movements, ability to move, to walk, are literally disappeared, made to vanish from the streets, from our communities, who were separated from the lives of others, quite possibly from their very own; to refugees who are told that their presence is, their very footsteps on lands are, illegal, who are thrown into processing centres, treated like non-humans, kept barely alive, just *bare life*; to everyday occurrences where some people are, where one is, told to move faster, move slower, to get out of the way.

Which is not to say that one should ever ask, have to apply, for permission to walk, or to stop walking: after all, it is — at least should be — one's right to move, to walk. But that even as walking, moving, movement, and thinking, are related, have a relation with each other, this relationship can be coopted, swallowed, perhaps digested, turned back upon us — where instead of choosing to move, we are moved, shifted, shafted; where instead of thinking, we are herded, flocked, maneuvered, into unthinking.[234]

---

[234] *Guattari discusses micro fascisms which exist in a social field without necessarily being centralised in a particular apparatus of the State. We have left behind the rigid shores of sentimentality, but we have entered a regime which is no less organised and where each embeds himself in his own black hole and becomes dangerous in that hole, with a self-assurance about his own case, his role and his mission, which is even more disturbing than the certainties of the first line: the Stalins of little groups, local law-givers, micro-fascisms of gangs ...*

~ Gilles Deleuze & Claire Parnet, 'Many Politics' in *Dialogues II*, translated by Hugh Tomlinson & Barbara Habberjam. New York: Columbia University Press, 2007, 138-139.

So, once again, *how might we give shape to that space, that place — that encounter — we call eating, being, with?*

And here, we should open the possibility that we might have been asking an erroneous question: not so much that there is a correct one (that would presume there are right answers, even worse single correct answers, which brings us back into an exclusionary, certainly inhospitable, state; moreover, despite Aristotle's exhortations of method, of *meta hodos*, one can never quite know where the top of the mountain is, or what a quest entails until undertaking it), so not so much that there is a right, even pertinent, question, but that — as the great Italian reader, writer, thinker, gourmand, Umberto Eco, continues to remind us, *intelligence also entails saying no*: though, I suspect, a *no* that is not an absolute rejection, nor a classic negation (it might be due to my lack of imagination, and *mea culpa* if so, but it is rather difficult to imagine either Georg Wilhelm Friedrich Hegel or Immanuel Kant losing themselves in sensorial pleasure), so and rather a *no* that suggests there might be a possibility of more, of other possibilities, perhaps of otherness, of a *strangeness* even; a *no* that isn't afraid to, as Avital Ronell continues to teach us, « plunge into the night of non-knowledge ».²³⁵

After all, as Avi also continues to remind us, « writing creates strange destinations and unassigned deviations, makes things happen and rouse out of a subterranean slumber ».²³⁶

Ah, to sleep, perchance to dream.

So, perhaps we could approach the question — *how might we give shape to that space, that place, that encounter, we call eating, being, with?* — from a slightly different angle, maybe even a slanty one (there might well be *clinamen* involved; for who can truly know if one comes to a thought, or if it swerves into one, there almost certainly entail accidents, perhaps even immaculate conceptions): where it is not so much how we might *give shape*, as if we are the ones responsible for

---

²³⁵ *To the extent that thinking plunges into the night of non-knowledge, a wide range of surprise attacks ensue, bringing about not only what oppresses, but also unanticipated délices, the tremors of sensation that incite newness, stirring everything that we can't be sure of—the unrecognizable, the future, mutations in being as well as unaccountable aggressions, the ceaseless dreariness of worry, or the dazzle of caress, such as Lévinas, Derrida, and Nancy spark off.*

- Avital Ronell, 'The Experience of Stupidity', *Electra — Contemporary Revolts* (Issue 2, Summer 2018).

²³⁶ This is a thought that first came to me while Avi and I were on one of our teaching-walks in the forests of Saas Fee, during a summer session of The European Graduate School, August 2007.

making this space, but as much about *getting out of the way* in order for this space to *shape itself*.

After all, the danger of eating the apple being not just that one has *knowledge of life and death*, but perhaps even more so that *one thinks one knows*.

Bearing in mind that to know is to be in the past.

So, always also *tell me what you have eaten and I'll tell you who you are*. Tell me *what has eaten into you* and I'll tell you who you are.

Or, maybe even, who you *were*.

So, always also a question of *what remains*.

If only you dare look a little closer, you might catch a glimpse of ghosts. Where you might have to, perhaps even literally, *eat your heart out*.

No one said that knowing — and if *an unexamined life isn't worth living* (trying not to forget that the last thing[237] Socrates ingested was what killed him) — so *living*, and more precisely *living well*, didn't entail risks.

After all, as the late great Anne Dufourmantelle, dear dear Anne, continues to teach us, « being completely alive is a task, it's not at all a given thing. It's not just about being present to the world, it's being present to yourself, reaching an intensity that is in itself a way of being reborn ».[238]

A rebirth that is not necessarily completely new (which is not possible) but a *new that is a same that is not quite the same* — or, as our Thai friends put it so much more beautifully, that is *same same but different*. Or, if you prefer a more European flavour (one should never ignore the question of preference, and of taste; after all we are in the realm of the senses, of *aisthesis*), so if you prefer a more continental palate, we could also say — by way of the particular, slightly

---

[237] In any earlier incarnation of this piece, I had a delicious typo — 'the last *think* Socrates ingested was what killed him' — which I was so tempted to keep (like Wilde, *I can resist anything except temptation itself*), but in a rare moment of propriety caved into the norms of privileging signification over pleasure. One does wonder though what his last think were about.

[238] Anne Dufourmantelle, 'The Ideology of Security', public lecture at The European Graduate School, (August 2011).

peculiar, French of Gilles Deleuze and Félix Guattari — that this is a rebirth due to an *intensity* that brings forth, even *cooks up*, a *minor literature*.

And here I'm not saying anything that you all — all you magicians and lovers of food — don't already know: for, what is a *minor literature* but a way of encountering something that opens oneself — and the thing itself, by relation that is; for all we can ever know of something is through ourselves in relation with it; where we are the very border, limit, threshold itself. And by opening ourselves potentially also engendering — at least momentarily — a slightly porous, slanty, swervy, possibly illicit, perhaps risky, potentially charming, relationship.

A boy can only dream.

Ah, an opening of ourselves — *as a space*, perhaps even as *spaces* — to encounter the world, in all of its vibratory potential, all of the possibilities that are already in there, but usually unheard, unseen, perhaps waiting to be seen, heard, touched, felt, lived.

whiter shade of pale, 2021

To see in an egg all of it possibilities, possibilities that are in it, in its multitude of forms: and, as importantly, to be open to the « ghost of future possibilities » in the egg, if we allow an echo of Mark Fisher to resound here;[239] future possibilities as ghosts of potential futures that have lingered with us, alongside unsatisfied possibilities, perhaps even actualisations that have not satisfied their possible potentials.[240]

---

[239] Mark Fisher, *Ghosts of My Life: Writings on Depression, Hauntology and Lost Futures*. London: Collective Ink (Zer0 Books), 2022.

[240] Not that we'll ever, or can actually ever, know what said potentials are; even after they might have happened.

So, not so much that we are remembering, as in recalling, them, but that the ghosts of memories themselves are calling out to us ... *remember me.*

En bref, « to », as William Blake reminds us again and again and again, « to see a world in a grain of sand / and a heaven in a wild flower ».[241] All whilst trying never to forget that it is *in* a grain of sand and not *in place of* it: the world was always already in place there.

If we pay attention.

And see both 'sand' and 'world', hear both 'heaven' and 'wild flower'; encounter both as *same same and different.*

If we attend.

Open ourselves: where shaping of spaces of hospitalities is nothing other than giving space — *giving ourselves into and as space —* for encounters to take shapes.

---

[241] William Blake, 'Auguries of Innocence', *The Pickering Manuscript.* Accessed at *Poetry Foundation.*

Even at the risk that *being well* and *living well* might
    sometimes

                  involve

                            falling

                            into

                            wells.

The so-called political-film has often seemed to me to have something Wagnerian about it, to produce the same effects Wagner inspired in Nietzsche: you recognise it as powerful but feel it is artificial, ponderous ...

~ ROLAND BARTHES

Neither painting nor drawing, nor art in general, can achieve anything. It is far removed from colonial appetites and does not even wish to beguile one's contemplation: art does not serve and there are no correspondences, intercessions, or contradictions to be found. This painting, this drawing, is entirely autonomous and engrosses the viewer in a vain search for analogies.

~ HUBERTUS VON AMELUNXEN

mother & child
— *a song, an ode, a eulogy* —[242]

You carry us, once upon a time within you, then on your back now where still we are. Floating across the tarmac of time, laid by those who first came, as we lie, staying as still as can be, holding, clutching clinging on, sometimes — often — in vain.

The last thing we want flung our way be the accusation of rocking the boat.

Regardless of whether it even be the same one: someone should ask Theseus. Though in this case, it would be difficult to ascertain if it be the planks that are exchangeable or us who are infinitely replaceable. *Same same but different.*

This contemplation will have to be left to one with time, a time belonging to them, who has the means to mark out a space for observation, carve out an area (oh my, real estate) for the taking of auguries (*templus*). So one that the divine will deign to speak to;

---

[242] This piece is inspired by *Shams*, an in-situ installation by Adel Abdessemed; « a work born from suffering ... a portrait of the 'damned' of contemporary times » (MAC Lyon, programme).

our profaneness already demarcating us.
Crossing temple thresholds requiring
freedom to make vows, votives, for devotion
... of time.

Our time, ours long already traded away
sold bought; all we can do is crouch, clock in
clock out as time clocks us, just hopefully
we've weaved bowed down enough to not
get knocked out flung off thrown out evicted
replaced effaced. Jumping to the beat of
another, dictated by some metronome.

殭屍.[243]

Time, one not on my side, in which they —
you, all of you — are free to make marks,
mark us out regardless of how hard we keep
our heads down, remark on us, mark us
down (oh how you all love marking and
marks here), even make your own mark, on
me.

Ours, oh ours, our hours, already etched
onto, indented into, us.

---

[243] *Zombie* in the Mandarin.

Mandarin is one of the four official languages in Singapore; the other three being Bahasa Melayu, Tamil, and English (which is also the official working language).

> *Mother, mother, how's the family?*
> *I'm just calling to say hello.*
> *How's the weather? How's my father?*
> *Am I lonely? Heavens know.*
>
> ~ Tracy Bonham[244]

•

8 December 2013, Little India, Singapore, 9:21 p.m., a fatal accident occurs at the junction of Race Course Road and Hampshire.

A few minutes earlier, Sakthivel Kumarvelu, a 33-year-old construction worker hailing from Tamil Nadu, attempts to board a private bus ferrying workers from Little India to their dormitory in Jalan Papan on the western outskirts of the city.

There are approximately 1.2 million migrant workers currently in Singapore making up around 38% of the workforce. Primarily from Bangladesh, India, and China, they work mainly in the country's low-wage sectors. Often reliant on

---

[244] Tracy Bonham, 'Mother Mother' in *The Burdens of Being Upright*. London: Island Records, 1996.

employer-sponsored temporary work visas, they live in constant uncertainty — at the whims and mercies of bosses who can fire you willy-nilly — and the risk of deportation.[245]

Mr Kumarvelu is denied entry on account of intoxication.

What else is there to do to forget? On your one rest day in a city where you have no family, nor friends beyond fellow indentured workers. And are sequestered into dormitories, away from the populus,[246] released once a week. One does drink to feel the waters of Lethe — and to feel alive, if only for a moment. What else is there to forget?[247]

---

[245] Amanda Oon, 'Remembering Singapore's Little India Riots' in *Southeast Asia Globe* (20 Dec 2022).

[246] Many of these dormitories, in which — although official figures are not disclosed — about 85% of migrant workers live, are « cramped, housing around up to 20 residents in a single room » (*ibid*). Beyond the inherent ethical problem of packing humans like sardines — sacrificing humanity on the altar of production, profit, surplus value — the dangers of this approach were laid bare during the COVID-19 pandemic where « migrant workers have accounted for almost 90% of the over 60,000 cases confirmed in Singapore. At the time, a humanitarian disaster seemed likely, with massive infection clusters emerging one after another. Fortunately, only 27 deaths [were] recorded ». (Song Yihang, *NUS Law*)

[247] There are varying accounts as to Mr Kumarvelu's level of drunkenness. Fellow worker Mr Ganesan Thanaraj, who was in the

The bus speeds off.

Mr Kumarvelu gives chase, catching up as it pauses at Race Course Road. He attempts to get on, slips. Falls under the wheels of the bus, they go round and round, round and round ...

Approximately 40 minutes later, his body is extricated by police officers.

Within minutes, around 400 members of the country's migrant community flood the streets in furious protest.

A fuse had been lit.[248]

---

same bus, testified in court that he « looked like he had been in control of himself » (Amanda Lee, *Today*, 25 Feb 2014); the bus operators had « asked him to exit the vehicle as they were not permitted to ferry drunk passengers » (Nadene Chua, *The Straits Times*, 11 Nov 2024).

Naturally, accounts, memories, perspectives — even motives and inclinations — differ. But perhaps the question which remains is: *who gets to decide?*, and *whose decision matters more?*.

[248] Under the *Criminal Law (Temporary Provisions) Act 1955*, strikes are illegal in Singapore for workers in essential services — with sentences up to a year in jail and a fine of 2,000 SGD — unless the employer is given 14 days' notice.

[Cheryl Sim, 'SMRT bus drivers' strike', *National Library Board*]

.

In the case of what has come to be called — more accurately, *framed* by the state media as — the 'Little India Riots', 25 people were charged, including instigators and those who were actively engaged in acts of

It would be more accurate to say it had been *re-lit*.

Only a year before, November 2012 it were, 171 bus drivers hailing from the People's Republic of China had gone on a two-day wildcat strike: protesting their salaries, deemed lower than those of drivers from other countries; and the standard of their accommodation — also sequestered dormitories — provided by SMRT Corporation, a subsidiary of state-owned multinational investment firm, Temasek Holdings.

Five drivers — Mr(s) Bao Feng Shan, Gao Yue Qiang, Liu Xiangying, Wang Xianjie, He Jun Ling — were jailed for between six and seven weeks, and 29 others were deported.

---

violence. 57 others — deemed to have knowingly joined or continued to participate in the riot, despite being ordered by the police to disperse — were deported and would not be allowed to return. Finally, 213 foreign workers whose involvement were assessed to be passive and incidental were issued warnings.

[Ministry of Home Affairs, 'Report of the Committee of Inquiry into the Little India Riot on 8 Dec 2013',57; Pearl Lee, *The Straits Times* (23 Dec 2013); Cheryl Sim, 'Little India Riots', *National Library Board*]

A fuse had been ignited.

•

And you run, and you run
To catch up with the sun, but it's sinking
And racing around
To come up behind you again.
The sun is the same in a relative way
But you're older
Shorter of breath
And one day closer to death.

~ Pink Floyd[249]

Now you always say
That you want to be free
But you'll come running back (said you would baby).
You'll come running back (I said so many times before).
You'll come running back to me.
Yeah, time is on my side, yes it is.
Time is on my side, yes it is.

~ The Rolling Stones[250]

•

Remember here, I am always two.

---

[249] Roger Waters, David Gilmour, Richard Wright, & Nick Mason, 'Time' in Pink Floyd, *Dark Side of the Moon*. Los Angeles: Harvest Records, 1973.

[250] Norman Meade and Jimmy Norman, 'Time Is on My Side' in The Rolling Stones, *12 x 5*. London: Decca, 1964.

No, not double, two.

All of you have at least two: the one through whom you arrived came to be; and the ones that you come to grow to learn to call end up calling acknowledging seeing as so.

Not necessarily separate, but perhaps never quite the same; *same same but different.*

> *Mother, do you think they'll drop the bomb?*
> *Mother, do you think they'll like this song?*
> *Mother, do you think they'll try to break my balls?*
> *Ooh-ah, Mother, should I build the wall?*
>
> ~ Pink Floyd[251]

Mother: the one watching over you, caring for you, paying attention to you, attending to you. Maybe even curating you, shaping, forming reforming you, quite possibly even deforming you.

Or not.

---

[251] Roger Waters, 'Mother' in Pink Floyd, *The Wall*. London: Harvest Records, 1979.

> Gaia, the name of a very ancient divinity, a Greek divinity much older than the anthropomorphic Gods and Goddesses of the Greek cities. It may be that she was a figure of the mother, but then not of a nice, loving mother, rather of an awesome one, who should not be offended, also of a rather indifferent one, with no particular interest in the fate of her offspring ... Gaia is this figure of the many figured Earth which demands neither love, nor protection but the kind of attention to be paid to a prickly powerful being
>
> ~ Isabelle Stengers[252]

Could well be a vessel; and you, a vassal. *I am your ship, worship me.*

Or not.

A passage through a birth canal need not take on any meaning; passing through doesn't mean that you weren't merely a passenger. You could have just been in transit; might well have been trying to go undetected. Just sliding by, justly, justifiably or otherwise. You often have to readjust when uninvited, when your host offers only limited extremely conditional hospitality. Where should you show, they think imagine you are displaying, any sign of turning from guest to invader, you are immediately

---

[252] Isabelle Stengers, 'Cosmopolitics: learning to think with Sciences, Peoples, and Natures', lecture at Saint Mary's University, Halifax, Nova Scotia, 8 January 2014.

regarded seen treated as hostile; and they turn kidnapper, taking you hostage.

*Unknown item
in the bagging area.*

One could always hope I am more Durga than Gaia. Nurturing. Caring. Protecting. Mothering. Even then, bear in mind I am also war, destruction, sometimes oftentimes in the name of righteousness, protection, liberation.

Not just that I can become both Devi and Kali.

I am both.

Always both and more so much more.

*Naming things is never innocent.
It is to precipitate them beyond their own existence
into the ecstasy of language which is already the
ecstasy of their end.*

~ Jean Baudrillard[253]

---

[253] Jean Baudrillard, *Cool Memories: 1980 – 1984*, translated by Chris Turner. London: Verso, 1990, 35.

Making oneself *impassible, invincible,* even *unassailable,* entails turning myself into a *fortress* (Durg, दुर्ग), fortifying myself, erecting walls borders gates reinforcements enforcements enforcings reinforcings policings permits classifications evictions exploitations deportations.

Turning oneself into a sarcophagus.

Container. Containing. Containment.

> *The form of the name*
> *— a place of solitary confinement —*
> *eats the body and holds it upright.*
>
> ~ Jacques Derrida[254]

And devouring the flesh (*sark-*) within.

You.

Keeping you on my back so on your own two feet — away — you will never walk.

•

---

[254] Jacques Derrida, *Glas*, translated by John P. Leavy Jr & Richard Rand. Lincoln: University of Nebraska Press, 1986, npg.

So, on our own two feet,
we cannot walk.

> *When you sent me off to see the world*
> *Were you scared that I might get hurt?*
> *Would I try a little tobacco?*
> *Would I keep on hiking up my skirt?*
>
> ~ Tracy Bonham[255]

There was a time I was more reckless with my heart. When I used to stroll, even saunter, around an area of town that purported to be a small even little — how cute — India. When I still could smile a wry smile at the ludicrousness of lumping almost 200 languages and close to 20,000 dialects into a monolithic whole. The white sahibs I can almost understand: they with the mien of, with their addiction to, arbitrarily drawing lines, splitting peoples families worlds in twain overnight at the strike of a pen. These people, they who claimed independence, who claimed to be free, *merdeka*,[256] to even sharing a continental

---

[255] Tracy Bonham, 'Mother Mother'.

[256] *Independence*, in Bahasa Melayu.

fraternity, that's a little harder to bear, to stomach.

Ah, a time when I would even drift, perchance to dream, on a sidewalk, imagining under these pavements lay a beach, *que sous les pavés la plage.*

Movement, ah moving, that you should never take for granted.

> *I'm hungry,*
> *I'm dirty,*
> *I'm losin' my mind,*
> *Everything's fine.*
>
> ~ Tracy Bonham[257]

Which is not to say that one should ever ask for, or have to apply for, permission to walk, or to stop walking: for, it is one's right to move, to walk, to have your feet touching to have the right to have your feet touch the ground.[258]

---

[257] *ibid.*

[258] For a longer meditation on *walking, moving,* and their potential relationships with *thinking, movements,* and *resistance,* please see my 'Walking with my friends', *Philosophy World Democracy*, 2021.

As we tried to state express demand plead cry-out on the night 8 December 2013. When we tried to say *we have had enough*. And, perhaps foolishly, certainly naively, dared to imagine that a country enraptured with the coming of Santa might have been feeling a touch of generosity.

We were met instead with Krampus.

And called — daddy called us — rioters.

*Naming things
is never innocent.*[259]

Quite apt perhaps: intergenerational love of floggings and all that. *Spare the rod and spoil the child*. As if we were children; I suppose it's always in the eyes of the beholder, it's easy to *see what you want to see, would rather see*. Of beating into shape. Being beaten into shape. *Daddy, daddy, tell me I've been good*. Accepting that it is one's lot to be shaped. *Hit me baby one more time*. Herdings, flockings, designings, with people imagining they are walking, moving, even thinking, freely when already being moved shifted shafted.

---

[259] Jean Baudrillard, *Cool Memories*.

To even thinking it be good to be shaped reshaped shaped-up. Terrified of being the square peg in a round hole. Shape me, reshape me, unshape me, make me, mis-shapen me, make me, *hit me baby one more time*.

After all, *the happiest slave be the one who thinks themselves free*.

> *I'm freezing,*
> *I'm starving,*
> *I'm bleeding to death,*
> *Everything's fine.*
>
> ~ Tracy Bonham[260]

So maybe it is not only I who have been put back on my back, on a flat bed, taken off my own two feet.

Maybe that's why my person — my *being* — be invisible to you all, merely a pound of flesh, not even, almost certainly less, just an image, yours of me. Not that you cannot see me, but that you have to see me there, there and only there. On her back, being ferried, feet firmly off the ground — your ground. Yes, there. There, I have to be, remain, stay.

---

[260] Tracy Bonham, 'Mother Mother'.

So you can tell yourselves you are not me.

•

26 February 2025, in response to a question from then-Member of Parliament Louis Ng — about feedback on improving safety for workers transported on the backs of lorries, and on even banning the practice altogether — Senior Minister of State for Transport and Sustainability and the Environment Amy Khor said, « for many micro, small and medium enterprises, it is neither practical nor viable for the employers to have different vehicles and drivers to transport a small number of workers separately from their equipment and goods ».[261]

Ah, Singapore, where everyone is but a resource — and movement, production, productivity, progress, be the order of the day. Commodities: not just constantly depreciating but exchangeable; when longer deemed useful, disposable.[262]

---

[261] Vanessa Paige Chelvan, 'Banning lorries from transporting workers not practical, could force smaller firms to shut: Amy Khor', *The Straits Times* (26 Feb 2025).

[262] "[Singapore needs] the 900,000 foreign workers on 2-year work permits. They do the construction and other heavy work, jobs

Wheels that keep on turning. Keep running, or fall off.

நாம் அனைவரும் வெள்ளெலிகள்.²⁶³

To mother, to care.

To curate, even be your personal curator for the times you fall, sometimes on your haunches, often off high horses, even the back of a truck.

To even be your hero.

But not just in any way, least of all mine. Less it be called smothering. Like when the Care Bears *stare*; you are never quite sure how much caring remains in that act of obliterating what has been deemed undesirable. We often kill what we purport to love protect defend. *Killing in the name of* ...

Singaporeans are not willing to do. Their 2-year work permits can be extended several times. *But they will not stay here permanently*." (Lee Kuan Yew, speech, *emphasis* mine).

²⁶³ *We are all hamsters*, in the Tamil.

And your remains can be trucked away. Or, put on a wheel (*trokhos*), and then made to run (*trekhein*) — run away as fast as you can. *You spin me right round, baby right round.*

And if not quick enough, a lorry will pull (*lurry*) even tug (*lurry*) you, your body, *corpus tuum*, in the direction deemed right for you.

Straight lines only.

Alas, people think protectors only turn into Hera upon lapsing. So easy, maybe more convenient, to forget that heroes all come from me.

And why, why should I be held to your standards? It is not as if curators, in the precise sense of one who cares (*cura*), have not slowly but surely died ... most everywhere ...

Swallowed by the rise of the salesperson (or *the gallerist* if you prefer the other name with which they go by). Which is no fault of the gallerist as such: after all they are merely living up to their call to *play to the gallery*.

> *Naming things*
> *is never innocent.*[264]

And, it is perhaps of no coincidence that galleries quite possibly bring with them echoes of church porches (*galilea*), albeit from afar (which might well be apt seeing that a *portico* is part of its structure) — after which, the *klang of coins* is never far behind ...

    ... render unto
    Caesar.

•

I would be deeply offended if you were to call what I do Sisyphean: that would imply previous wrongdoing ... unless you too consider being poor a crime.

And, do please bear in mind that it be my flesh that is being consumed. *Hoc facite in meam commemorationem.* Which might be why I have to be housed apart so you aren't constantly reminded of your cannibalism.

And why my movement needs, *every step I take, every move I make* — and we need — to

---

[264] Jean Baudrillard, *Cool Memories*.

be put on display, on show (*montre*), to be staged (*theoria*) every morning, every evening.

> *Society desperately needs monsters*
> *to reclaim its own moral virginity.*
>
> ~ Sylvère Lotringer[265]

Not just for yourselves: *be assured, they are always in transit, only temporary. Breathe in, breathe out, sun salutation, child pose, child pose, breathe, breathe ...*

But also for us: be constantly moving in constant motion so you never forget you are transitory, infinitely replaceable, temporarily housed, that despite having built most of this city it will never be home. *Wise men say, only fools rush in ...*

---

[265] Sylvère Lotringer in conversation with Johnny, as quoted in David Wojnarowicz, 'The Suicide Of A Guy Who Once Built An Elaborate Shrine Over A Mouse Hole' in *Close To The Knives: A Memoir Of Disintegration*, with an introduction by Olivia Laing. Edinburgh: Cannongate Books, 2016, 202.

> *Who loves, trembles*
> *for the other, by the other.*
>
> ~ Hélène Cixous[266]

Though, it's not as if you will ever be rid of me: me, I have already written myself into your buildings.

No wonder you seem so eager to knock them down.

> *Am I in love? — yes, since I am waiting. The other one never waits. Sometimes I want to play the part of the one who doesn't wait; I try to busy myself elsewhere, to arrive late; but I always lose at this game. Whatever I do, I find myself there, with nothing to do, punctual, even ahead of time. The lover's fatal identity is precisely this: I am the one who waits.*
>
> ~ Roland Barthes[267]

•

---

[266] Hélène Cixous, *Animal Amour*. Paris: Bayard Éditions, 2021, 40. (translation is mine).

[267] Roland Barthes, *A Lover's Discourse: fragments*, translated by Richard Howard. New York: Hill & Wang, 1978, 39-40.

Mother, should I run for president?
Mother, should I trust the government?
Mother, will they put me in the firing line?
Ooh-ah, is it just a waste of time?

[...]

Hush now, baby, baby, don't you cry.
Mamma's gonna make all of your nightmares come true.
Mamma's gonna put all of her fears into you.
Mamma's gonna keep you right here, under her wing.
She won't let you fly, but she might let you sing.
Mamma's gonna keep baby cosy and warm.

[...]

Ooh babe, ooh babe, ooh babe.
Of course, Mamma's gonna help build the wall.

~ Pink Floyd[268]

---

[268] Roger Waters, 'Mother' in Pink Floyd, *The Wall*.

As we go across the Benjamin Sheares bridge, me bearing your weight on my back, feeling the road beneath me, I can see the city gleam before my eyes, sunlight flickering from the glass kingdoms scraping the skies. Today, the sun seemed to be streaked with sunlight.

It could have just been my tears.

> One can testify only to the unbelievable. To what can, at any rate, only be believed; to what appeals only to belief and hence to the given word, since it lies beyond the limits of proofs, indication, certified acknowledgement [le constat], and knowledge. Whether we like it or not, and whether we know it or not, when we ask others to take our word for it, we are already in the order of what is merely believable. It is always a matter of what is offered to faith and of appealing to faith, a matter of what is only 'believable' and hence as unbelievable as a miracle. Unbelievable because merely 'credible'. The order of attestation itself testifies to the miraculous, to the unbelievable believable: to what must be believed all the same, whether believable or not.
>
> ~ Jacques Derrida[269]

This being the risk of opening my mouth, of drawing attention to myself, instead of just *keeping your head down, putting your back in it*, and going home when done, really *when we're done with you*.

Here, wrung out any morsel of life from you in you.

For, whenever you testify to something, what you are really doing is asking for others to *believe you*, to have faith in *you as you*: you

---

[269] Jacques Derrida, *Monolingualism of the Other; or, The Prosthesis of Origin*, translated by Patrick Mensah. Stanford: Stanford University Press, 1998, 20.

are doing nothing other than putting your very self, your body — and if you'll allow me a little homonymic mischief here, *your testes* — your being, on the line.

Giving you a chance to cut them off.

Maybe this be your way of making us a little more like you, *descendants of the eunuch admiral.*[270]

---

[270] *Descendants of the Eunuch Admiral* was written by playwright, director, intellectual, and activist, Kuo Pao Kun. The work critiques contemporary culture and the required castrations (and silences) required to get ahead, to *majulah** as it were.

In March 1976, Kuo was detained under the Internal Security Act for alleged communist activities and had his citizenship taken away in 1977. He was detained for four and a half years and was released with conditions in October 1980. The restrictions were withdrawn in 1983 and his citizenship reinstated in 1992.

[Marsita Omar, 'Kuo Pao Kun', *National Library Board*]

* *Majulah Singapura* — 'Onward Singapore', from Bahasa Melayu — is the national anthem of Singapore. In many ways it captures, even exemplifies, the state's obsession with *moving forward*, sometimes regardless of cost, or upon whose backs this so-called progress is made.

As we were carried across the Benjamin Sheares bridge, us bouncing on your back, feeling the city, what I still think is my city, vibrating through you, I can see her gleam before my eyes, sunlight flickering from the glass kingdoms scraping the skies. Today, the sun seemed to be streaked with sunlight.

It could have just been my tears.

twenty twenty-three[271]

the only thing that
continues to surprise me
is that we are still

surprised that we still
continue to claim to be
surprised each time this

happens as if the
surprise would save us having
to acknowledge that

we would much rather
remain surprised than to not
devour prizes

peoples lands so *this
is no doubt a perfectly
ordinary year*[272]

> *I wake up in the morning and I wonder
> why everything's the same as it was*
>
> ~ Skeeter Davis[273]

---

[271] A version of this work was first published in *positions* in December 2023, and republished in *Poiesis: A Journal of the Arts & Communication*, Vol. 21, 2024: 167.

[272] closing line to the poem '一九八九年' by Yang Lian, translated into the English as '1989' by Brian Holton.

[273] Sylvia Dee & Arthur Kent, 'The End of the World', single by Skeeter Davis, New York: RCA Victor, 1962.

What I saw, heard, learned, from Plato's style: that philosophy needs myth not because the latter is closer to truth, but on the contrary, because myth is indifferent to both truth and falsity. Myth is the antidote to the word's presumption to utter propositions that are solely true (or solely false). If what is at stake in a proposition is the idea, then it is impossible to demand that it be either true or false, as Plato's shrewd disciple was wont to do. The only discourse that is philosophical, Plato suggests, is a discourse that contains its own mythical complement, and can therefore proclaim both 'the truth and falsity of being as a whole'.

~ GIORGIO AGAMBEN

It has to be said that writing is an inhuman and unintelligible activity — one must always do it with a certain disdain, without illusions, and leave it to others to believe in one's own work.

~ JEAN BAUDRILLARD

in case[274]

and everything is green and submarine, 2022

on occasion when possible I write
not in capitals — for certainly am not
certain enough to sentence sentences
to death

might though have to resign myself
to the thought that each reference to my-self
— every time my hand inscribes an « I » — entails a
suicide note

---

[274] A version of this work was first published as 'Cases' in *RIC Journal* in January 2023.

being encased in cases

the convergence with myself I find uncanny
knowing me and not I alternately simultaneously
recovering one and losing the other — memories
they be tracing themselves into us springing
themselves on us when and as they choose to
sometimes

invisibly

but perhaps with a certain care even
a certain care not to care a care not to
certainly care I shall let my thinkings rest
just so I might remain

in case

Art and order,
the relatives that refuse to relate.

~ ELFRIEDE JELINEK

I'm just a writer.
Either the songs come or they don't.

~ PHILIPPE ROBRECHT

Given that there is world that side of the window
and world this side, perhaps the I, the ego, is
simply the window through which the world looks
at the world. To look at itself the world needs the
eyes (and the eyeglasses) of Mr Palomar.

~ ITALO CALVINO

In our haste to measure the historic, significant, and revelatory, let's not leave aside the essential: the truly intolerable, the truly inadmissible. What is scandalous isn't the pit explosion, it's working in coal mines.

~ GEORGES PEREC

Even if the world's beauty and love were on the edge of destruction, theirs would still be the side to be on; defeated love would still be love, hate's victory would not make it other than it was.

~ SALMAN RUSHDIE

Jeremy Fernando reads, writes, and makes things.

He works in the intersections of literature, philosophy, and art; and his, more than thirty, books include *Reading Blindly, Living with Art, Writing Death, in fidelity, Tómate un paseo por el lado oscuro del camino, resisting art, Writing Skin, A Ghost Never Dies, The feather of Ma'at, i'm not ghosting you, I wish we were lovers*, and *Jeremy Fernando by Jeremy Fernando*. His writing has also been featured in magazines and journals such as *Arte al Límite, Berfrois, CTheory, Cenobio, Entropy, Full Bleed, Poiesis, positions, Philosophy World Democracy, Queen Mob's Teahouse, Qui Parle, Testo e Senso, TimeOut*, and *Voice & Verse Poetry Magazine*, amongst others; and has been translated into the Brazilian-Portuguese, French, German, Italian, Japanese, Korean, Spanish, Serbian, and Turkish. Exploring other media has led him to film, music, and the visual arts; and his work has been exhibited in Seoul, Vienna, Hong Kong, Lisbon, and Singapore. He has been invited to read at the Akademie der Künste in Berlin in September 2016; and to deliver a series of performance-readings at the 2018, 2020, and 2022 editions of the Bienal de la Imagen en Movimiento in Buenos Aires, the latter at which he also curated a filmic omnibus entitled *reading dreaming malaya*.

He is the general editor of Delere Press; curates the thematic magazine *One Imperative*; is the Jean Baudrillard Fellow at The European Graduate School; co-creator of the private dining experience, People Table Tales; and the writer-in-residence at Appetite, the sensorial laboratory exploring the cross-roads of food, music, and art.

Sometimes, the world leaves you temporarily helpless and unarmed. Stories leak away and you're left with a profound silence. You have to wait until the words and the images come back to you.

~ MIKE CAREY

What exceptional good fortune to be a South American and specifically an Argentine and not feel obligated to write seriously, to be grave, to sit in front of the typewriter with shined shoes and a sepulchral notion of the gravity-of-the-moment. Among the lines I most precociously loved as a child was one spoken by a classmate: 'What a laugh, everyone cried.' Nothing is more comical than seriousness understood as a virtue that has to precede all important literature (another infinitely comical notion to hear proposed), the seriousness of the person who writes like someone obliged to attend a wake or to give alms to a priest.

~ JULIO CORTÁZAR

La peinture: des ruissellements, des surgissements, des rapprochements possibles entre l'idée, la chose, la permanence de la chose, son inanité, la matière de l'idée, de la couleur, de la lumière, et Dieu sait quoi encore ...

~ MARGUERITE DURAS

www.ingramcontent.com/pod-product-compliance
Lightning Source LLC
Chambersburg PA
CBHW041039050426
42337CB00059B/5058